The Novice Is Missing . . .
And So Is
the Convent Bike!

Katey Moreland

WORD of the LORD Wine Press

Published by WORD of the LORD Wine Press
Limerick
Ireland
Email: wordofthelordwinepress@gmail.com

The publishers aim to produce books that will build up the Body of Christ, encouraging a fresh filling of the Holy Spirit, hearts revived in the love of Jesus and lives restored to Kingdom principles. We do not necessarily agree with every view expressed by the author or with every interpretation of Scripture made. We expect each reader to make his/her judgement in the light of their own understanding of God's word and in an attitude of Christian love and fellowship.

Photo on front cover used by permission, © Winnie Blaney

ISBN: 978-0-9575494-0-1

Cover design by Jim Weaver Design Ltd
Typeset by CRB Associates, Potterhanworth, Lincolnshire
Printed by TJ International, Cornwall

Many Thanks:

To **Holy Spirit** – *Teacher, Friend, 'God's gentle dove',*
*To **Jesus** – holding my hand, daily affirming God's love,*
*To **my Father** – 'silent' in my broken, hurting world,*
Working 'behind the scenes' to restore His 'little girl'

*To **Yvonne**, **Penny** and **Filis** –*
Saving me from cracking-up, if truth be told,
Escaping in laughter –
Out of the belly, relief to the soul☺

Joyful melody bursts forth from a grateful heart
To a lady 'there for me' from the start,
Showing love and commitment, no matter the strain,
Supporting me as I dealt with my pain.
A life fully-blossoming began with sharing;
*My dear **Sister Caris**, thank you for caring!*

*Thanks ascend to **my special Sisters** residing in glory –*
Their unconditional love toward me
Makes this – my life – their story!

Contents

Acknowledgements 6
Note to Readers 7

1. In the Beginning Was the Word 9
2. You Shall Know Them by Their Fruits 21
3. You Will Find Rest for Your Soul 37
4. Your Healing Shall Spring-forth Speedily 53
5. A Time to Gain, a Time to Lose! 65
6. Be Filled with the Spirit 77
7. The Silver-Haired Head is a Crown of Glory 89
8. Confess Your Sins to One Another 101
9. His Grace is Sufficient! 111
10. Be Kind to One Another 123
11. Blessed Be God! How Wonderful Are His Ways! 141
12. Ask and You Shall Receive 153
13. In the Multitude of My Anxieties, I Put My Trust in You 169
14. I Love You with an Everlasting Love 187
15. My Presence Will Go with You and I Will Give You Rest 205

Useful Information 221

Acknowledgements

My special thanks go to the Sisters with whom I spent my formative years for giving me such an interesting tale to tell! Thanks to Sisters who read and approved my story. Thanks also to those who contributed to 'Footnotes of Fairness' and those who gave permission for their 'fun photos' to be in this book.☺

Thanks also to friends, Sr. A, Krys, Bridie, Siobhan, and Mary, for reading the manuscript and giving helpful critical appraisal.

Thanks to Julie Maria Peace for her outstanding kindness – and keen eye – in proofreading most of my book. With the shortest of time available she, like God, has proven she can do the impossible!

Thanks to my cousin, Winnie, for taking the front cover photo.☺

Thanks to everyone whose advice helped to choose the best book cover possible!

Thanks to friendly critics for raving reviews.

Note to Readers

This is my story – or should I say, the story of my younger self! The facts and feelings are *'true'* as I remember them, re-enforced by extracts from my *Letters to Jesus* journal and little book of reflective poetry, as well as letters received from my mother. Location and character names (including my own), however, have been changed for privacy's sake.

I present the story from my younger-self's outlook without necessarily agreeing with her thoughts, feelings or behaviour. How much less, then, can I expect the Sisters with whom I shared those years to agree with her perspective! I have, therefore, given them a 'right to reply', recorded on the relevant pages in *'Footnotes of Fairness'*.

I hope you enjoy☺

Katey Moreland

1. In the Beginning Was the Word

There she stood at the bedroom door, my arch-enemy, grinning ear to ear like a Cheshire cat. Towering over me, holding a wet pair of briefs in her hand, she peered down and asked, 'Did you drop these on the stairs?'

I blushed as I reached out to accept my washed laundry. Olive Oil skipped down the stairs with obvious glee at putting the novice in her place. My arch-enemy was no less than the Novice-Mistress, and was not really called Olive Oil, but named so by Yvonne and myself when we joined the Novitiate on account of her lanky legs and disastrous social skills that enabled her, like Popeye's girlfriend, to tie herself in knots.

If you've wondering what on earth a novice and Novice-Mistress are, let me explain. The definition of a novice, according to the dictionary is 'a probationary member of a Religious Order', or in my simple language, 'a trainee nun'. A Novitiate is a house where trainee nuns and their Novice-Mistress live, and the Novice-Mistress, according to my then-juvenile definition, is 'the nun who gets to control the novices' lives'!

'How did my life come to this?' I cried out for the millionth time.

I had begun a personal relationship with Jesus as a teenager four years earlier and professed I would do anything for Him. When I was two years old in the Lord, and still a teenager in the natural, Jesus had revealed He was sending me to be a Missionary in Africa. Thinking He meant immediately, I replied, 'But Lord, I have no experience or qualifications. Who would accept me?'

Not much later, an advertisement from the Children's Rescue Society immediately caught my eye,

'You don't have to go to Africa to be a Missionary.
Come to Chester and help take care of children'

The advertisement offered the opportunity of a year's voluntary work in the Society's homes and nursery, each participant provided with accommodation and pocket money.

Reasons for wanting to participate were listed:

- Test a vocation you might have
- Experience community living
- Gain experience in childcare

I didn't mind experiencing community living, but my main reason for applying was to gain experience in childcare, and I most definitely did not have a vocation to become a nun! I made sure I informed the interviewing panel – if finding a nun was to be their number one factor for accepting applications, they should choose someone else – I most definitely did not have that call! Apparently, as I left the room, Fr. McKieran, the Head of the Children's Rescue Society, and the Sisters on the interviewing panel agreed, 'She's the one that will enter at the end of the year!'

I, of course, knew nothing of their prediction, but it wasn't very long before I started to 'get the call' – not a call I wanted, by the way! Up until then, I would spend hours alone with Jesus in the chapel in the evenings. However, when the 'call' began to sound, I began to run! I'd be so quick to get out of God's presence that I'd leave my Bible behind! When I'd return an hour later, I'd make some excuse, 'Sorry, can't chat, got to dash!'

Of course, God was everywhere and could speak to me anywhere, so I always had to be on my guard, keeping my mind and hands busy. Eventually, however, I was worn out from running, and sad not to be in close relationship anymore with my First-Love. Still cringing at the thought of becoming a nun, the chapel now seemed such a foreboding place to 'chat with God'. Yet, still wanting to hear His voice, I decided I'd go to a place in which I could be comfortable enough to let God speak. Taking a train on my day off, packed-lunch in my backpack, I headed out of the city and into the countryside. Reaching the woods for the first time, I embraced my exploring adventure with excitement. I was full of praise for all the beauty I saw – 'My Lord made that!' The hours passed and I was glad to be in fellowship with Jesus once again. Then, as I turned a corner to see a high set of stone steps, I knew the moment had come – time to let God have His say! We climbed the steps together, stopping on each one – God had something to say. I listened. I wanted to object, but stayed silent. Besides, God could hear my heart – Please, No!

Step-by-step, God worked on convincing me,

'I have called you; you are mine.'

'I send you to the Nations.'

'My plans for you are for good and not for evil.'

'I love you with a never-ending love.'

I had counted the steps – probably in the hope of drowning out God's voice! – As I reached the fortieth and final step, I succumbed, not to pressure, but astounding love.

'Okay, I'll do it!'

I returned to the other girls in our home in a wealthy suburb of Chester with the knowledge that I was about to embark on the biggest change of my life, yet told no one. In a couple of days time we would each be returning to our family homes for a holiday – I would take my secret home with me to check it out away from 'community living'; maybe, just maybe, I hadn't heard God's calling, but being around the nuns from morning to nightfall was having an adverse effect on me! Yet, no sooner was I home than I was telling my mum I was joining the Sisters. Momma begged me to reconsider. Not that she minded me becoming a nun, but wanted me first to take up a place offered in Theological College. Her suggestion sounded wise, but after months of struggling with God's request, my adamant reply spilled out of my mouth, 'No, Mum, you don't understand – I have to obey God!'

Before leaving home, as much as I believed this was God's call, I instinctively rebelled, asking the hairdresser to turn my brown locks into baby-pink spikes. I would shock the Sisters into refusing me entrance!

On our return to Chester, we were to pack-up and head-off again taking a trip to France and Spain. I, of course, needed to speak with the Mother Superior about 'my calling'. With no time for an office visit, any discussion would have to be during our travels. The coach had barely begun rolling along when I was told to go and sit with Mother Anastasia for a chat. I still had in my mind that if I appeared too outlandish, she would reject me – in a kind way, hopefully, saying something like, 'That's very interesting – maybe you should go and do something else, dear, and come back to us in a few years!'

Sliding down the seat to get comfy, my knees leaning against the seat in front, jaw busy chewing gum, I began my story, interspersed with bubble-blowing, of how God had spoken to me in the chapel, how I hoped the notion would go, but no, it remained. Mother Anastasia, attentive to my words, didn't seem to notice my appearance or behaviour! Recognising her to be a 'cool cucumber', I even wondered if she would still not have flinched if I had put tattoos all over my face! Mother Anastasia began talking about me entering the convent, perhaps in September, as another candidate was ready to enter too. My face began to burn and my ears began to pop – I could no longer distinguish the sounds coming out of Mother Anastasia's mouth, but after a few minutes, the hand gestures suggested our conversation was over. I returned to my seat and with a look of shock told my friends, 'Oh now I've done it – she's accepted me!'

Cheers went up, especially from Cath, a 'Lancashire lass', but I sat, mummified – had I really given my life away so easily? And yet, strongly desiring to please my God, I could see no alternative!

Having finishing my 'voluntary year', I returned home in perfect timing to join the youth from church in going to see the famous American Evangelist, Billy Graham, leading a Youth Meeting in Bramall Lane Stadium in Sheffield. My nine-year-old nephew, Peter, like a little brother to me, was by my side and filled me with such joy when he joined hundreds of others on the football pitch to declare he wanted to receive Jesus into his heart. His adult life might not yet have much to show for his decision – oh, but it will! He and his wife have a mighty future in the Lord's service, beyond my level of courage! Soon receiving apologies that my date for entrance was delayed, I arranged a trip to Rome to visit a Sister I had met when she visited Chester. Mum was anxious for me travelling on my own. Then I got a phone call with a new date of entrance – September 25th 1985.

'No!' I cried. 'That's the week I've booked a flight to Rome to visit Sister Rose-Anna.'

Mother Anastasia graciously found a solution. 'As you're with our Sisters on that date, you can enter in Rome.'

'Cool – thanks!'

Another visit to my local hairdresser in Yorkshire was needed before I headed off to Rome. 'Be as daring as you like – I'm on my last fling!'

Leslie cut my hair short on one side of my face, leaving it long on the other side with a slope in between. I loved it, feeling years ahead in 'trendiness'!

'Now for the colour – I'll be the only one without a blue veil on my big day, so go ahead and turn my hair blue – make me fit in!'

Sister Rose-Anna was anything but pleased when she welcomed the new recruit to Italy and was extremely annoyed when we walked the streets of Rome – on account of all the young men on mopeds honking their horns! Turning around to see me smile, she angrily asked, 'Are you sure you want to be a nun?'

Being so close to Assisi, Rose-Anna thought the atmosphere of St. Francis' hometown might tame my spirit! I wasn't so sure – wasn't Francis a radical in his day, choosing to sleep in woods and meadows instead of his family home, and even refusing to wear appropriate clothing! Yet, one thing was for sure, the day trip would be a wonderful 'entering' gift, and make the day unique. I had already thought it sounded grand to say I was entering in Rome; now I could say I also entered the convent in Assisi – how many Sisters could say that!

The next day Rose-Anna took me to the Vatican for an audience with Pope John Paul II, even having a photograph taken with him – a gift I was sure my Momma would love. How wrong can you be?

'He's staring at you like you've got two heads!'

'They're not used to dyed hair in Rome', I explained.

I thought I was 'saved by the bell' as the phone rang out in the hall, but instead – eerily – the caller turned out to be Mother Anastasia desiring, it seemed, to add to my birth-mother's correction: 'Welcome home! I am told you had a nice time in Rome – and you've been somewhat expressive with your hair. I trust that's all washed out of your system now, and you will present yourself as a Sister should!'

'Yes, Mother', I replied, somewhat sheepishly.

So that was it! On my last night, Mum arranged a lovely surprise party at the church, after which I packed my belongings and the following morning headed towards the old train station in Rotherham. My Momma and sisters waved me off as if they'd never see me again, yet I was only going as far as Chester, for now at least. Before becoming a novice, I was to live in community as a 'postulant' or candidate – before getting into the real training of the novitiate for a period of eighteen months, a six month period is given in which one tries out 'community living' while the Sister-in-Charge assesses your suitability. I was grateful my first month should be with Sisters I knew in Chester and trusted Sister Caris, as Sister-in-Charge, to give me a kind report☺. The taxi driver, however, was shocked to hear a young, bubbly girl was about to enter the convent,

'Ere', he said, removing a magnet from his dashboard, 'a customer gave me this prayer to St. Anthony (patron saint of lost objects). You need it more than I do!'

Life was good in the convent in Chester – I loved baking, and landed a job in the kitchen. Father McKieran, eating my homemade apple pie commented that I made perfect puff pastry. This made me puff up with pride – I knew if I was to make a good nun, I'd have to work on that area of my character – but, oh well, plenty of time for that in the Novitiate, enjoy the praise for now!

One day I went shopping with Jackie, an ex-volunteer from a previous year, buying the loveliest baby-pink silky pyjamas, which Jackie agreed were 'classy'. However, on the return journey, sitting on the bus, she asked did I think I would be allowed pink silky pyjamas – I was, after all, supposed to be a 'trainee-nun' now! I wanted to do things right, so on meeting Sister Caris, I nervously asked was I allowed, expecting to be told to take the pyjamas back.

Sitting in her navy blue habit, she smiled and answered, 'Of course, you're allowed. There's no colour-code on your nightwear.'

Still feeling nervous and thinking about the sackcloth Francis wore in his vow of poverty, I asked, 'But is it too nice?'

Sister Caris laughed. 'You're allowed nice things.'

Turning to her desk behind her, she reached out her hand to a small white bottle decorated with hazy pink flowers. 'Here's some perfume my sister gave me. I don't wear much perfume – but I could if I wanted to. Here, you have it – enjoy!'

I still enjoy wearing Anais Anais today – from a different bottle of course!

My month in Chester was over all too soon and I must go to Brighton Hall in the Cotswolds donated by Mrs. Brighton to the Sisters decades before. I had visited twice previously – once with the volunteers and once after I had 'received the call'. On our first visit, a hush came over the mini-bus as we descended the long drive toward the Tudor 'mansion' decked in black and white. Never had we seen a house so striking or vast – and we were invited to sleep there! On my second occasion, I slept in a guest bedroom above the chapel. The journey itself to the bedroom was quite an experience – up the grand stairs and through rooms of oak panelled walls. Even before I saw the luxurious king-size bed, I could have wondered if I was in a convent or five-star hotel. Everyone had been so lovely on that visit, putting me at my ease. On my first day, as I nervously walked along the corridor to the office I met a sweet-natured, well-spoken lady, Sister Juliet, who, like every Sister before her, welcomed me to Brighton. Asking my name, she replied, 'Oh, *beautiful* – it means *Pure*, you know?'

I didn't know; in fact, I was amazed! Didn't I feel so impure, and longed to be pure – 'that's my name?' I wondered incredulously. When I was seven, the priest's housekeeper took a photo of me on the day of my first Holy Communion writing on the back, **'May our Heavenly Father keep you always as pure as you are this day. God loves you'**. At the time of the photo, I was a cheeky little madam, no doubt about it, but my purity was intact. There was a smile within me at Sister Juliet's news – humanly speaking, Mum had chosen to name me after a nurse who thought I was adorable, but God had purposed to call me 'Pure'! All nervousness regarding my 'new life' dwindled; Jesus was going to make me pure again, Alleluia☺ On that visit, however, I had not met the Novice-Mistress – it was Wimbledon fortnight, the weeks she always took her annual leave.

Now it was October, and I, with the falling leaves, must leave the security of the tree to which I felt grafted to join the community in which I must receive most of my 'formative training'. 'Calmly' sitting at the train station waiting to be collected, suitcase and teddy by my side, no one would know moving to Brighton Hall was, for me, the most frightening ordeal! The house was beautiful – the gardens within the estate and the surrounding area were stunning, even a dream come true to live in the countryside, but was what I believed of Olive Oil true – a tyrant who would soon whip me in to shape? Fortunately, I still had a number of months left as a postulant; Olive Oil could not yet take control of me! Even before becoming her 'charge' I hated being in her company, feeling under constant judgement – was my very persona despised, as I so strongly believed, or was my fear of rejection from those born 'above' my working class roots colouring my judgement? Sister Juliet talked as if she had a plum in her mouth, obviously from a 'well-to-do' family, yet I loved her company for the tone of her words toward me was always so kind and gentle. Setting the tables with her one evening in December, Sister Juliet began to tell a story to share what the Novitiate was like in the 'old days'.

'We each were assigned an 'angel' when first entering the Novitiate to take care of you. I was appointed your Novice-Mistress's angel. One day I took her to the Grotto.'

I quickly responded, 'You should have left her there!'

Little titters could be heard as Sister Juliet lifted her hand-kerchief gently to her mouth to muffle the sound of laughter while she collected more plates from the trolley. Sister Alison, practising on the organ for the Christmas concert, turned her head to face us and solemnly announced in her monotone voice, perfectly befitting a late night horror movie, 'Beware; novices have been strung for less!'

Her words, and the way in which she said it – slow and meaningful – made me shudder inwardly, but, ever the performer, I answered playfully, 'Good job I'm not a novice then, isn't it!'

Sister Juliet tittered as she moved on to set the next table but Sister Alison shook her head in disbelief before resettling herself at the organ, purposefully holding down the lowest key for a number of seconds. I knew her unique recital held a warning: *my words would come back to haunt me!*

Not yet being novices invited into the Novitiate, and no longer guests who could enjoy the luxurious guest suite, we were moved into the stables – phew, talk about following in Jesus' footsteps! – Well, not actually stables, but stables converted into flats. We lived in the apartment downstairs and the Convent priest, Fr. Smith, lived in the apartment upstairs.

'The good old days' in which the other postulant, Yvonne, and I had many a midnight party – howls of laughter as we ate delicious puddings sneaked from the kitchen and listened to favourite music. Likened to two cheeky monkeys by some of the Sisters, we rehearsed many a sketch to entertain them in this our fun-hour. Apparently, Fr. Smith did not mind our creativity, just the time in which we chose to express it!

'It sounds like there's a whole gang of them down there', he complained to one Sister, 'but I'll leave them be; they'll face the wall soon enough!'

You've heard of 'Reprieve on Death Row'? Our 'facing the firing squad' was delayed by two months as Mother Anastasia, needing to go abroad on urgent business, was unable to be present on the original date set for our entering the Novitiate. Yvonne and I were sent off to other community homes to gain further experience, I going to Liverpool to help the Sisters in a retirement home for priests. In working hours, I especially liked being in the laundry away from the main house and turning Pirate Radio up to full blast. A forest nearby, running alongside the beach, protecting red squirrels from the vicious grey ones, became my favourite place to retreat in the afternoons, but I also enjoyed living in this small community. They were all so welcoming, friendly and full of fun – not that the Sisters in Brighton weren't, but here I was free from judging eyes. In my determination to enjoy my escape, I could blossom. By the time Mother Anastasia came to visit Liverpool, one Sister had taught me to knit, another all about the beauty of Kenya, and a third how to put and take off skirts correctly (put the skirt on over your head, and take it off around your ankles – there, now you've learnt something new!) Obviously, now I was ready for the Novitiate!

If only! The moment Yvonne and I arrived in the Novitiate our lives completely changed; a lead weight kept us grounded whenever we entered the little cottage at the end of the grand estate. Olive Oil was going to keep us in check for nineteen months.[1] Yvonne and I agreed, even this small incident involving my underwear was a reminder of that fact!

'C'mon!' Yvonne jumped to her feet, 'let's go for a bike ride before prayer-time.' We put on our tracksuits and headed for the bike shed.

As we spun around the country lanes, Yvonne bellowed, 'Remember, when she gets too much for you, you can always escape on the convent bike!'

At suppertime that evening, Olive Oil, the Queen of Implication, explained that due to the fact that some Sisters in the Mother-house in Chester jogged outdoors in tracksuits she could not stop us from wearing tracksuits, but would prefer us not to. We nodded to show we understood before lowering our heads to take another bite of food, side glancing at one another before sharing a secret grin – if she couldn't make us stop wearing our tracksuits we'd keep on wearing them!

---

[1] **Footnote of Fairness:** Much of 'Sr. Peter's' emphasis as Novice Mistress was on 'character-forming' as it would have been before the reforms of Vatican 2 (1962). This may be seen as controlling to young women in the 80s. (Sister Representative)

2. You Shall Know Them by Their Fruits

When my birthday arrived at the end of April, we had been living in the Novitiate less than a month, awaiting our official entrance into Sisterhood in a few more weeks, yet our two week holiday in March to mark our end of Postulancy seemed but a distant memory. For my time at home, I had chosen to block out fear that attached itself to my entering the Novitiate, determined to enjoy visiting with family and friends. Momma, so generous a giver and lover of 'a good knees-up', arranged yet another surprise party for me – this time an early birthday gift, which was absolutely wonderful, but my brother Chris's children all had to remain home with Chicken-pox, three year old twins Jonathan & Antony, and baby Ryan being especially weak. They didn't have the energy to play the usual games of football outside or hide-and-seek indoors, but just wanted to snuggle-up like little kittens and be caressed in their discomfort.

Soon it was time for me to go back to Brighton – absolute trepidation was in my heart as I got on the train. Could I really survive the Novitiate? Arriving, Olive Oil showed Yvonne and me upstairs to our rooms – both back rooms, overshadowed by the woods, so no great light would ever be revealed there! Diagonally from the room allotted to me another room shone so brightly, drawing me close – could I not move into that one?

'No' came the polite reply, 'but you can watch the sunrise from there – as long as you wear your bedroom slippers.'

O.O's instructions seemed strange to me, and her refusal unfair, but Sister Nora, a novice for almost eighteen months, now ready for 'escape' through profession, was given the unenviable task of explaining Olive Oil's thought patterns. 'She doesn't let anyone stay in that room because it's above her own. If ever you do go in, you mustn't make a sound; she doesn't like to be disturbed!'

Watching Nora intrigued me for she had learnt exactly how a novice should behave and seemed like an angel, gliding from room to room with a holy glance on her face. I knew I could never be like that!

In my 'new home' neither the bathroom upstairs nor the toilet downstairs had windows but were equipped with a fan light. Going to the bathroom within an hour of arriving, the noise of the fan caused severe pain in my head. Holding my head in my hands, I despaired. 'Oh, LORD, I can't stick this – how am I going to survive this place if I can't even go to the toilet in peace!'

That night, I woke from my sleep with an even worse headache accompanied by nausea, not only that, but my whole body was covered in spots; I had caught Chicken pox! The following day the Doctor made a 'home call', prescribing painkillers and camomile lotion.

Did I understand I could not go over to the main house or go near any of the older Sisters?

'What???' – My only security in this place to be taken from me? This cannot be happening to me!

Apparently, the older Sisters could get shingles if they had contact with me. O.O informed the Doctor, an elderly Sister, Stevie, resided with us. 'She should move out – just to be on the safe side, at least for the first two weeks.'

Oh, no, not Sister Stevie as well! How long must I be confined?

'The infection normally lasts for two weeks, but I'd like you to be excluded for at least three weeks, to make absolutely sure. I'll come back and check you then.'

Then, as ill I was, I had what I considered a great idea – let only the young ones remain!☺

'You're getting on a bit, aren't you Sister – don't you think you should go over to the main-house too?'

O.O scowled at me before raising her voice an octave. 'No dear, I'm the Novice-Mistress. The Novitiate cannot operate without me.'

Smiling sweetly at the doctor, she turned to take out her frustration on my bedding, tucking me in tighter than a strait-jacket. 'Besides dear, you need me!'

We soon found out the stage of nausea had not fully passed as breaking free I bolted upright and reached for the bucket!

My Momma soon wrote, asking me how I was for spots, and shared how my brother Chris and his wife, 'had a good laugh' when they heard I had caught Chicken Pox! Their eldest daughter, nine-year-old Clare, excitedly claimed, 'I gave them to her.' Over the coming months, Momma's letters would tell me which child in the family was the latest to catch them, slowly making their way around the whole clan. For the first few days, I was very weak so my enforced exclusion passed me by without a great deal of upset, but my lack of energy was a great frustration to me. I practically lived on soup, unable to hold anything else down. On the fifth day, I purposefully slept for two-and-a-half hours after lunch to build up enough energy to take a half-hour walk, but on reaching the Novitiate gate, I needed to return to my sickbed! The following week, with more energy, I began to take strolls in the gardens. I felt like a leper though, all but taking a bell with me shouting, *'Unclean, unclean!'* if an elderly Sister happened to walk in the same direction.

In the second week, Sister Greta celebrated her Golden Jubilee, which meant everyone, besides little lonesome me, was over at the main house. Amidst the list of attendees from outside Brighton convent, Yvonne spotted Sister Jean's name – a lovely, bubbly Sister living in Chester. Although no suggestion was made, I was sure Jean would come over to visit me. I sat in the living room, reading my books, listening to the wall-clock count time, periodically checking over the hedge for movement, expecting at any moment the gate would fling open and I would excitedly meet Jean at the front porch. I wouldn't even go out for a walk in case I missed her! However, the hours began to pass by – late afternoon; could she still be there? After a long afternoon, the wanderers returned – in time for evening prayers. Still I looked beyond the three bodies residing in the Novitiate to the door behind them –

'Has everyone gone home?' (Praying desperately inside the answer would be 'no')

'Yes', came the cheery reply, 'Sister Jean brought these cards for you, but you'll have to read them later. Now it is time for prayers.'

As I dutifully ascended the stairs, disappointment completely deflated me: how could she know I was ill and not come to see me! (The thought that she wouldn't be 'encouraged' to visit never entered my head!) I couldn't even stir up appreciation later in the evening as, sitting alone in my bedroom I read the lovely greetings from 'friends far away'. Opening my little book of plain lilac pages entitled 'Recollections', I began to scribe:

> *Oh, dearest Jesus*
> *What is your plan for me?*
> *What do you want to happen?*
> *Why can't You let me see?*
>
> *And why must I stay here?*
> *Why can't I be moving on?*
> *Locked up in here alone,*
> *The trees even keep away the sun!*
>
> *I receive no body,*
> *Or blood shed by You,*
> *But, dearest Jesus,*
> *I know your love is true!*
>
> *So won't you give me Bread,*
> *Bread from Heaven above,*
> *To fill my heart, Jesus,*
> *With Your everlasting love?*
>
> *Take me in Your arms, Lord,*
> *And teach me How to Love,*
> *So that I may trust You*
> *To be my reigning 'Gov'.*
>
> *And couldn't I just love You*
> *And accept the pain within;*
> *No visitors for a week or so*
> *And not even a proper din'!*

As everyone went to bed after night prayers I sat in the twilight, only one candle flickering; all was calm, all was still – the only answer that came to my heart was I must put my disappointment to sleep; before long, I would be free again!

When we realised my birthday would fall in the period of confinement, Olive Oil suggested with so much free time on my hands, I bake my own birthday cake. Finding her suggestion unbelievably insensitive, I stubbornly dug in my heels; I would rather go without than bake my own gift (which is exactly what happened!) My response did not help Olive Oil's assessment of me. She had no grave concern about Yvonne's suitability as a candidate – Yvonne was mature and possessed reasoning skills, yet I was still a juvenile – a most unruly one at that – my training would take great scrutiny if the Novice-Mistress was to succeed! I was continuously bombarded with instructions on 'correct behaviour'; first came instructions through implication from Olive Oil, and then explanations were given from Nora. Before long, Olive Oil dropped into conversation another hint of expectation; although blue clothing was not compulsory until we were officially novices, it was preferred. Although I had all my 'nun outfits' up in my wardrobe I refused to wear them until I had no choice. Being as defiant as ever, I immediately rang home asking Mum to send my big huggable blue and white striped cardigan and blue hippie skirt interlaced with gold, red and silver threads from which hung a multitude of little brass bells. (*That'll show her!*☺)

My birthday arrived before the clothes did. I was allowed to go to Mass as a 'birthday treat', but must arrive long before the others, sitting in the balcony, and wait until the Sisters had disappeared before I should descend the stairs again. Seeing them from above made me miss them even more! On my return to the empty Novitiate, Jesus gave me a birthday gift, as remains our custom today. Usually, Jesus gives me a Scripture, but on this occasion, He spoke directly into my heart:

'All is still and I lie in that stillness, come abide with Me.'

Replying to Jesus' invitation, I wrote:

> *'Be still' is your command. I understand. I'm to come to the quiet, learn to be quiet, live in the quiet. 'Be still' means leave all their worries to themselves, too. Instead, I treat the 'quiet' as a problem. When I first began to tackle the problem of my being 'loud', I didn't even know I had a problem! Each day I find out more about myself. My loud ways are a tonne weight and I want to throw them out of the window but in so trying I fist bang all the furniture and then I accidently smash the window. If I ever got so far as to throw my tonne weight, it would make such a crash that my loud ways would still be with me!*
>
> *Lord, I treat the quiet as a problem; I want to reach it today, but it has to be gradual. Yet I don't even begin the transformation; all I seem to do is recognise myself. Others will have seen that person from day one. I'm eternally grateful for their company. It's a wonder I wasn't left to be a hermit long ago! My searching explains why the old are described as 'wise'!*

When the clothes arrived later that afternoon, everyone presumed the parcel was a birthday gift. I said nothing, scampering to my room to open the parcel, still planning to go ahead with my plan, 'fighting on' even though Jesus asked me to 'be still'! In the middle of the parcel, I was delighted to find Mum had kindly put in two boxes of chocolates. Opening one box as I descended the stairs, I stopped to 'savour the flavour' of a 'melt in your mouth' experience. Offering chocolates to Nora and Yvonne as I entered the community room, Nora, who was kept very busy, informing me of all my 'wrong behaviour', gasped, 'You're not allowed to open gifts of chocolates and sweets. You give them to the Novice-Mistress and she brings them out on a Feast day.'

'You're joking!' I insisted, stuffing another chocolate in my mouth.

'Can't she just tell her she didn't know', Yvonne asked, wanting to defend me.

'No, she does everything by implication – you're supposed to know you're not allowed!'

My only response to such confusing rules was 'Eh?'

'What's all this commotion?' Olive Oil waltzed into the room before Nora could explain further.

Olive Oil shifted her eyes between the half-eaten box of chocolates and my full cheeks.

Nora began to explain nervously, 'Sister, I was just telling Kaitlyn that she's not allowed to open chocolates, but she didn't know.'

'We were just talking about what we should do', Yvonne added.

'You give them to me, that's what you do', Olive Oil demanded, snatching the chocolates from out of my hand. Appearing to mellow a little, she continued, 'We shall eat them on a chosen feast day.'

'Well, seeing as that box is open', I argued, 'can't we eat that box and keep the other for a Feast Day – be a pity to waste them!'

'They won't be wasted – they'll keep!'

And with that Olive Oil waltzed back out of the community room and into her bedroom. *With my chocolates,* I thought, *I bet she's eating them right now!*

That evening, long before the others joined me for night prayers, I sat in the Novitiate chapel, a small room with kneelers placed in neat rows instead of seats (except one chair was put in for Sister Stella –she was after all in her seventies!) As Nora came in, followed immediately by Olive Oil, I wasn't sitting on the kneeler, but sat cross-legged, my legs totally covered by my skirt, only my pink fluffy slippers protruded out, left and right, from under the skirt. My Bible sat comfortably between my knees. Nora's eyes bulged out at me, trying to warn me with her gesture, before taking her position on the kneeler before me. Hopelessness filled me within; what impropriety was I committing now? Before Olive Oil took her position, she glanced down at my lower body, and then up to my face to give a look of disgust. I looked myself over – I was dressed decently, so that wasn't it – I must be in the wrong position! Obviously, kneelers were provided, kneelers should be used! After the prayers were complete, the Sisters began to file out. Olive Oil and Nora stood outside for a moment. Amidst the nods, Nora glanced back through the glass panelling in my direction still sitting in the chapel, before Olive Oil descended the stairs leaving the mature novice alone on the landing. Nora then came back into the chapel, sitting quietly beside me. Whispering, she told me I must never cross my legs in chapel or wear slippers. I was furious!

'I was just told to inform you', Nora gently reminded me – the blame was not hers!

'I know', I agreed, trying to hold back the tears.

With that, Nora bid me 'goodnight', reminding me novices should be in their bedrooms with lights out by 10.30p.m. In my fury, I marched off to my bedroom next door, dressed for bed and ranted and raved before my God for two hours. I could not calm down enough to sleep and so, collecting my journal, fully clad in pyjamas, dressing gown and pink fluffy slippers, returned to the chapel and, in a cross-legged position, began writing:

Dear Jesus,   *30.04.86*

Here I sit at 12.12a.m. with my legs crossed before you. Are legs so ugly that they should not be crossed before you in the Chapel? Can't You accept me as I am? Am I not to be myself – even before You? Am I not to sit comfortably? Am I crucifying you by a mere position? Is it irreverent? Isn't it the heart that matters – the within position? Do I really have to change all my ways?

In everything I do, and everything I say, I recognise myself as working class. Am I to become middle-class to become Christ-like? Do you say, 'Yes, I want to save you, but you have to become middle-class first'? Didn't you come to birth in a lowly stable? Did the shepherds have to clean themselves up before they could enter into your presence? Did appearances matter, or was your message the very opposite?

*'We shouldn't wear bedroom slippers before the Lord'! Do you 'pigging' care about what are on my feet? Are you as hung-up on appearances as people are? Or is it true that you said, 'I do not judge as people judge. Man looks at the outward appearance, but I look at the heart' (in 1 Samuel 16:7). **Is it true?** Does God still think like that? Yahweh, God the Father, said it long before you came on this land to show man's customs were not the Law of God. The Jews were looking at appearances instead of being concerned with the heart. And what do Christians do – decide to follow You but take upon themselves more man-made customs than your teachings!*

Jesus, if Religious life means becoming a middle-class idiot, a hypocrite, I want out! I just don't want to know, Lord!

Weren't You the only one to see my chicken-pox all over my body? Is it a simple box for our soul or should we take such great care of the box, doing everything correctly so that we come to admire the box and our efforts, that we forget the soul, our prize possession, needs all the attention we can give. Shall I stop praying while I'm in the bath, never to meditate again? Shall I ask you to wait outside while I sing my praises loud enough for You to hear? Or are you the All-Wise, wonderful God I think You are, who not only allows me to be as I am, but wants me to be as I am before You?

I'm sure when Mary Magdalene sat at Your feet, in true love and admiration, many people would have looked on in disgust – **'Look at her lording herself all over Him. She says He is truly from God; her actions don't seem to support her thoughts. Some people never change!'**

But to You Lord Jesus, appearances don't matter. Unlike the foolish onlookers, You see her intentions. You understand her every thought and action. You love her and You love me too!

I love You, Jesus, and I thank You . . .

After a few minutes of sitting in Jesus' presence, soaking in His love, I calmed down enough to write:

Jesus, how can You want me? How can You love me? I'm nothing but trouble! Although there is nothing wrong with wearing slippers or crossing my legs, you are not so concerned about the rules but my attitude. Your word says, 'Pray for those who mistreat you' (Luke 6:28b, GNB). Jesus, teach me to do what I must do in gentleness!

Later that morning the doctor visited, giving me the 'all clear' to return to the main-house. Too excited to walk, I ran all the way! I had loved the elderly Sisters from the minute we began to relate; my exclusion had brought a deeper appreciation of them and now I was determined to love them more than ever! As I entered the building, most of the Sisters were sitting in the dining room for 'elevenses'. If I had returned from Australia, I would not have received a greater reception; welcome cheers rose up and those with able bodies moved toward me, smothering me affectionately with hugs and kisses. I was in my element!☺

Of course, no such affection awaited me in the Novitiate! I resented what I perceived as Olive Oil's obvious dislike of me and in preparing for our lesson, I also prepared for battle; shoving to the back of my head my request from only twelve hours before that Jesus should teach me to behave gently, I returned to my bedroom to dress in my 'blue outfit' sent from home. My chunky blue and white cardigan, large enough to wrap around me twice hung loosely over my hippie skirt, the gold, red and silver threads shimmering amidst the dangling bells tinkling as I descended the stairs. On my entrance into the community room, Olive Oil, poor woman, nearly blew a vein out of her neck! After the teaching, I was kept behind and taken into Olive Oil's study, (no one is taken into her study!)

'Now, look here! Mother Anastasia warned me about you – that you were off the rails and needed to be brought into line. Well, I'm warning you – you either begin to behave exactly as I expect or you leave. Do I make myself clear?'

I left Olive Oil's office shocked and embarrassed by the direct correction and criticism. Yvonne was waiting for me and together we walked the grounds. I shared what had been said and then – shock of all shocks – Yvonne agreed with Olive Oil; my attitude was immature! For the rest of the walk, we walked silently. As we arrived back at the Novitiate, I burst into tears.

'We better walk around again', Yvonne calmly advised, shielding me with her body from prying eyes in the Novitiate. Eventually I conceded, 'I've realised I want to be a nun! Until now I've hoped to be sent home, but now I realise I want to stay and obey God's call. I'll have to tow the line and behave myself!'

In the movie *The Stepford Wives* the free-thinking women had to have their brains tinkered with to become 'perfect wives' but it took only one rebuke for me to vow that I would become the perfect novice. The transformation would astound them!

In my journal, later that night, I wrote to my Saviour,

Dear Jesus,

*I give you permission to break me, enabling you to remould me, but I want to know You love me. **You, Jesus, do love me!** That's all I'm sure of now. And I do marvel – why do You love this arrogant, selfish person that I wasn't aware of? It's a mystery to me, but please promise me You will **LOVE ME** forever and a day!*

I thank You for Olive Oil for being 'so blunt', as she put it. I thought I could sail through the Novitiate, changing in my own time without any outside pressures. I simply wanted to change through prayer, but I could have that experience in a bed-sit! I have decided to say 'Yes' to Your calling, to live in community, so I should live in community, give to community, be for community!

*I have a strong will, but I have been using that characteristic wrongly. I've been fighting against God and myself instead of for God and thus, for myself. My pride wants me to remain the same because I don't want Olive Oil claiming, '**I've changed her**', but I should know You and I alone are the one's who can change me! It's up to me to take the advice and work strenuously, unceasingly, with my strong will*

to become the person God wants me to be and the person I
want to be! God and I will have won the battle, no one else!

In Olive Oil's candid assessment of me, she had said many
things, one of them being she did not believe I had a vocation.
I knew the only Person in the whole world who could tell me
if I had a vocation was the One who calls, so I asked, as is my
custom, for Jesus to speak to me through the Word of God.
Praying something as simple as *'Lord, tell me what You think'*,
I open the Bible apparently 'randomly', but in essence not so,
because Jesus chooses the page at which it opens and where
my eye should glance. I have heard arguments that this is an
unacceptable method of communication with God or that it
is okay for 'baby Christians' but not mature Believers. May I
always remain childlike in this part of my relationship with
Jesus, for believing I have always received a direct answer!
On the question 'Am I called to remain or do I leave?' Jesus
gave the answer:

> 'The teachers of the Law and the Pharisees are the authorised
> interpreters of Moses' Law. So you *must* obey and follow
> everything they tell you to do.'
>
> (Matthew 23:2–3a GNB, emphasis added)

The word confirmed for me what I already believed in my
heart – God had called me to be in the convent. Not only that,
but again my Saviour was asking me to change my attitude
and behaviour, becoming obedient to those given authority
over me. I replied:

Olive Oil says she has been given orders from above to change
me. I shouldn't feel sad that Mother Anastasia wants me
changing; God above, Jesus Christ, who loves me through

*and through, wants the new me to appear! There should be
no embarrassment when someone says 'she's changed'. That
is the task in life, an ongoing change. We all change, but I'm
too loud to go unnoticed! Quieten me down, Lord, please.
Teach me to be conscientious, so that my words and actions
bear fruit – the fruit of hard labour and crucifixion, the fruit
of my King, fit to be presented to my King!*

In my little book of 'Reflections', I also wrote to my Saviour:

*Jesus, will you love me forever and a day;
    For My sins a high price You were willing to pay.
Can You dispel my darkest fears,
    Holding my hand until the light reappears?*

*Will you slowly show me my duties
    Planned uniquely for me,
To mould, to change, to love
    the real person I am to be?*

*Will You stay throughout the night
    Helping correct every error
        And protect me from the hidden terror?*

*Are you the Jesus I believe in –
    The One who conquers all sin?
You saw today's commotion –
    Lord, think of all that loose emotion!*

*Must I always end April this way
    To overshadow my special day?
I mark an anniversary with an other;
    Lack of understanding makes us suffer.*

In my heart of hearts, I knew my problems in the Novitiate did not stem from a dictatorial Novice-Mistress, as I claimed to anyone who would listen, but from my own stubbornness. My sister-in-law, Sally, turning up on the scene when I was only ten years old, accused me of 'inverted snobbery' – rejecting people from classes above my own on the basis of their upbringing. 'Reject before being rejected' was my reasoning. Knowing my self-protective attitude was forming a gulf between my Novice-Mistress and me, I wrote one final request before sleeping:

Oh Lord, that I could be wise enough to look below the surface and to love the real individual as you do!

3. You Will Find Rest for Your Soul

On 20th May 1986, Yvonne and I woke to the day in which we would officially join the Novitiate – I had made it without being thrown out! At breakfast, sitting in our best outfits, I found being filled with a mixture of anxiety and excitement left little room in my tummy for food and so just took a glass of water. Our invitation into the Novitiate was a small ceremony and the celebration modest, but no less significant for it. Back in the Novitiate after lunch, Yvonne and I stood at the bottom of the stairs awaiting O.O's directions.

She mistook our uncertainty for disappointment. 'I know it is rather deflating to have the ceremony and then return to the Novitiate to hum-drum living, but in eighteen months you'll have the big ceremony and you'll be off' (waving her gangly arm in the direction of the gate).

We smiled demurely, trying not to be discouraged by the reminder of our time 'behind bars', before being awarded a lesson-free afternoon to celebrate. I ascended the stairs thinking on my new name – Sister Mary Kaitlyn. In 'olden days' all sisters took on the name Mary, but that rule had long changed. I had been christened Kaitlyn Mary. Seeing Mary the mother of Jesus had chosen to put God before herself in answering His request to conceive and bear the Son of God, Jesus, I wanted her name before mine to remind me to do the same. When she said, 'Let it be to me according to your word',[1] she was truly laying down her life, accepting numerous times people would point the finger or ostracise her. Joseph had the right to have her stoned for mysteriously becoming pregnant during their engagement; even when he received revelation from God, think how many others would refuse to believe in a virgin birth! Yes, I too wanted to lay down my life for my God:

My dearest Jesus,

*Hello! Today is the most wonderful day in my life. Today I have become Sister Mary Kaitlyn. I have been chosen. That fact is very special in my heart today. You Lord chose me; You were never forced in any way; I'm not the only person in the world. You chose me from millions. I stand before you, before the Trinity, in amazement – God so big and I so small! You didn't notice me for my mouth or my bad manners, but something deep down attracted You – a seed You planted, which you want to nourish. Please, Lord, let it grow like an overgrown garden. Replace my whole being with the seed of Your love, let my life become one of love so that it is **'not I that live, but Christ in me'**. I want to follow Christ crucified. I want to be a martyr. I know I aim high, Lord, but You can teach me. If we start with little things (which will seem so big to me), we can gradually move on to bigger things.*

---

[1]   Luke 1:38

All these years later, I would not remember my desire for martyrdom, or the request I made, except I read it in my journal. Moreover, when I consider the proud way in which I so often behaved, the Sisters would not believe it either!☺ Nonetheless, my prayer continued:

Lord, what I'm asking for is the grace to love You so much – above humans or possessions – I want to share in Your suffering of the crucifixion, to suffer Your pain in the great cause of saving Your people. I couldn't follow You to the cross now because I love myself before loving You. I am so self-centred. I ask on this special day, You clear my centre of self and fill me with love of You, the Christ who willingly suffered on our behalf. Please, Jesus, allow me to follow in Your footsteps!

Having expressed my heart to Jesus, I turned to open the congratulatory cards handed to me by Olive Oil – even though they were from Sisters I had just spent the morning with, everything must now be done 'correctly' – they had given the cards to the Novice Mistress and O.O gave them to me! It was no coincidence that two cards held the same message:

'Take My yoke and put it on you, and learn from me, because I am gentle and humble in spirit, and you will find rest.'

(Matthew 11:29 GNB)

How I struggled with that verse! Through the eyes of self-rejection, always feeling my character was criticised by people, I was only able to see one message within Jesus' words: *What's wrong with you – why can't you learn to be gentle and lowly!*

I perceived God correcting me like a parent frustrated with His child (or a Novice-Mistress aggravated by her novice) – my brash nature was unacceptable, and oh, whenever would I stop being so proud!

I wanted to be gentle – in fact, I longed to be gentle, and was drawn to gentle people in the hope it would rub off on me! That's why I loved the elderly Sisters so much. Not all had attained it – a few were harsh! – But most knew a level of contentment that oozed out of them in varying degrees of peace. At mealtimes in the dining room, I would chat with the conversationalists, laugh with the jokers, and argue with the antagonists, but that would be 'relationship' for the external eye to see. Within, my heart sought out the gentle ones – I sat in their presence in the same way one might sit in a rose-garden, breathing in the scent, hoping to carry the memory amidst one's daily living. I longed to emulate their gentleness – and beat myself up every time I failed!

My over-desire to emulate one gentle lady many miles away was all mixed-up with my need for healing. Only weeks before receiving Jesus' invitation to learn directly from Him, I wrote about the greatest blockage I would ever suffer, deterring me from drawing close to my Saviour:

I can trust female friends because they're women, but You made Yourself Man. You are God, but You made Yourself Man, so I can't trust You! I want her to give me the love of God. Will she do it? No, never! Can she do it? No, she's not God! She's a very beautiful person, full of Jesus – but that doesn't make her Jesus! She is a human being, just like any other human being; she has failings like the rest of us! I know that Lord; I've known it all along – in my mind. But my soul, my will – I still will her to represent You Jesus, because she's all I hope you to be – kind, generous, considerate, humble, and so very lovable.

My knowledge of You, Jesus, is so limited; I know You love me and You have called me to You, but I don't really know You and I'm very frightened! It's like delving out into the darkness from underground. The light underground may be imitation, but it's safe; I feel secure! I've heard if I will travel to the surface, after the darkness comes light, much more beautiful than this imitation light, but I'm too afraid! I can't go through the pain of the tunnel for a man. And I can feel you scream out in pain in Your time of Your Passion, and Your Passion touches me very much, and I'm so grateful to You. You are God, You are Love, but You are man in my eyes, as is the Father – a most frightening word! Every time I begin the tunnel journey, I become aware of your Manhood. Godhood is overshadowed. Jesus, this is my greatest problem! Without passing this obstacle, I shall never be able to travel. I shall never be able to love You fully! I shall always be underground seeking the imitation light. As much as I've thought this through Jesus, I cannot sort it out! Only You can sort it out, Lord. Will You, Jesus – will You teach me to love You for who You really are – God! I know it's the devil whispering in my ear, reminding me all the time You're man to deter me from my journey, but I want You to teach me to believe that You are God – God who is to be trusted! Enter my soul, Lord, and teach my will to believe!

Painful relationships in childhood are often the root of our distrust in God. The person given the greatest responsibility of revealing the character of Father-God to me had instead made me recoil in fear and hostility. Only months after I had become a Christian, Mum asked me, somewhat cynically, 'Now you've become this new creation, I suppose you're willing to forgive your dad?'

For the life of me, I could not understand my mother's attitude toward my father! Almost two decades later, whilst receiving Christian counsel, I would see a vision of myself in the womb, little fists ready to punch the 'loud mouth' giving my mother verbal abuse. When I asked Mum why she had always spoken so positively of our father, she replied, 'He's your dad!'

Mum didn't need a psychology degree to know our identity, in part, comes from our parentage – she would make us feel as comfortable as possible with our genealogy. Faced with the question of forgiving my father, I was a million miles away from being ready to release him, but wanting to save face regarding my 'new faith', I gave the *correct answer* rather than the truth, 'Yes!'

Then thought, *Oh no, now he's going to visit and I will have to be nice to him!* He hadn't visited for a number of years. Whenever he had visited in years gone by, I wasn't free to tell him I didn't want to relate to him, so just made the excuse I was far too busy; homework and piano practice never got so much attention! Now, I'd be left with no excuses; I would have to relate!

My anxious concern was interrupted – alleviated – by the news, 'Good – because he's gone to heaven.'

My mother received no reply, but inwardly I declared bitterly, *'Fat chance!'*

Of course, I wouldn't know his 'chance' of entering heaven – he could have accepted Christ into his heart before being faced with eternity and like the criminal on the cross, be told by Jesus, 'Today you will be with me in Paradise'.[2]

I was but a few months old in Jesus when Mum and I had that conversation and four years old when I wrote to Jesus

---

[2] Luke 23:43b

about my fear of Father. Scripture says God is not slow to act, but gracious toward us. He waits for us to be ready to receive His good gifts. He graciously waited until I was ten years old in my spiritual life, knowing only then would I be ready to embrace healing and deliverance, and with it a brand new beautiful relationship with my Father in Heaven – Father God! In September 1991, I heard the most compelling message on the power of forgiveness – it doesn't so much set the offender free (he must still stand before God for all he's done), but it releases the offended one to live again. At the end of the message, I felt conviction to answer the altar-call. Standing in the queue, moving slowly toward the team praying with people at the front of the hall, I encouraged myself, *'I must forgive; freedom awaits me!'*

Receiving prayer, I immediately was 'slain in the Spirit'; falling gently to the floor, I began not only to declare forgiveness toward my father for incidents in my life, but also any I knew of in my mother's and siblings' lives. The list was long, my words deliberate, my voice aloud. Taking a break from the strain, I would interlude with a deep desire, *'I want to fly like an eagle!'*

A lady walking about, praying for those receiving ministry from the Lord, responded with certainty, *'**You will** fly like an eagle!'*

Even whilst I was there on the floor, releasing a catalogue of offence, my spirit began to soar; in the midst of the forgiveness toward my earthly father, without conscious decision, I began relating to Father God with the same love and confidence with which I related to Jesus. My new life beginning ten years earlier when Jesus and Holy Spirit came to dwell in my heart, was now truly complete, for Father God, the authority of the Godhead, who was also my Protector, my Strong Tower and my Refuge, was invited into His rightful place along side His Son and Spirit. In that moment, the head-knowledge that Jesus' sacrifice on the cross allowed me to enter the Most Holy Place became a living reality – bounding into Father God's presence, I jumped on the knee of the King as only a young princess could!

Of course, back in my convent days, I was too afraid of the image of Father to enter into the most amazing relationship there is, but God is gracious to wait! Silent in my broken hurting world, my Daddy was working behind the scenes to restore His little girl. Meanwhile, even though filled with fear of 'Man', I loved Jesus and held a deep desire to learn directly from Him, and to a degree I did, but for the degree I couldn't, Jesus had healing in His wings awaiting me. Throughout my life, as I embarked on a new chapter, Jesus repeated the same message as the day I became a novice. As I began healing and deliverance training fourteen years later with Ellel Ministries,[3] each member of staff was allotted a student to pray for, being instructed to send a welcome card with a scripture inscribed within. Sure enough, I opened the card to read,

'Take My yoke upon you and learn from Me for I am gentle and lowly, and you will find rest for your soul.'

(Matthew 11:29)

What was my response?

Despair! I still believed God was telling me I was too rough and proud. I knew that I knew God loved me so much, but I still struggled with rejection – big time! Rejection came in three categories – 'past rejection', 'self-rejection' and, the one controlling my every move, sitting in an imposing armchair

---

[3] Contact details are on 'Useful Information' page

in the corner of my living-space, remote-control in hand – 'fear of rejection'. I knew God loved me, but in the area of gentleness and humility, I believed He was telling me I failed Him! The enemy went as far as telling me I would never change and in never changing I would never be of full value in whatever ministry God would call me; my brash pride would damage whatever good I might achieve!

Within the next number of years, though, Jesus would take me aside to teach me so much about His character, healing not only my memories but my perception. In 2009, as I began a new ministry designed by the LORD, to travel Ireland with the message of unity in the Body being an important key to Revival, I once again received the message:

> 'Take My yoke upon you and learn from Me for I am gentle
> and lowly, and you will find rest for your soul.'
>
> (Matthew 11:29)

My goodness, how differently I now see Jesus' request! Thank God for His persistence! I spent my formative years trying to emulate gentle people, hoping to learn from them *how* to be gentle. Jesus says, *'Learn from Me'* – only He can teach me deep within my heart. Even being ready to receive healing took a lot of years, a journey of many miles, but in my Lord's healing grace I can now come to Him and commune with Him, and in that fellowship, learn from Him – a learning that transforms me without striving, just by being in His presence! I can learn much from being with the Master – if I want to heal the sick, I can learn from the Master; if I want to cast out demons, I can learn from the Master; if I want to understand the Scriptures, I can learn from the Master. When Peter and John spoke so boldly and eloquently to the Pharisees, revealing great understanding, the Pharisees realized they had been with

Jesus.[4] Michel Thomas, a famous language teacher, says learning is not the responsibility of the student, but the teacher. How much greater then is the promise of our Teacher, for when Jesus says *'learn from Me'* it means we are given the capacity; according to His grace, to become like Him!

Learning from the Master is key – you can learn through other people and their lives, but don't limit yourself to learning from them alone. 'A disciple is not above his teacher . . . it is enough that a disciple be like his teacher.'[5] If you learn only from man, you can only ever hope to attain what they attain – you can go no higher, and chances are, you won't even reach as far as you're aiming! So learn from the Master, that you may reach very high – as high as God would have you reach.

Without rejection acting as a lead weight to keep my eyes from lifting my vision higher, I'm free to consider Jesus' whole command. Jesus begins by telling us we must *Take His yoke upon us* in order to learn from Him. In farming, a yoke is placed upon working animals to steer them. You would never yoke together an ox and a mule – they're too different to have a successful partnership. There needs to be an equality in size and strength, even temperament, for the yoking together of two animals to be effective. Amazingly, the Son of God invites us to share a yoke with Him! How can that be? **It's all about God's grace!** We love God because first He loved us. We can come to salvation because we're invited. It's none of our doing and all of God's grace. Jesus comes alongside us and says He will make us as strong and powerful as He, but we need to realise His strength is in gentleness and humility.

---

[4]   Acts 4:13
[5]   Matthew 10:24a–25a

'Learn from Me for I am gentle and lowly' – Does it not seem
a contradiction to us that Jesus, who fought hard with the
Pharisees and cast out demons at every corner tells us He is
gentle and lowly? Jesus was as gentle as a lamb and as fierce
as a lion – work that one out!

Part of the answer is in Isaiah 42 foretelling of Jesus, the
Servant of the LORD,

'Behold, My Servant whom I uphold,
My Elect One in whom My Soul delights!
I have put My Spirit upon Him;
He will bring forth justice to the Gentiles.
He will not cry out, nor raise His voice,
Nor cause His voice to be heard in the street.
A bruised reed He will not break,
And smoking flax He will not quench;
He will bring forth justice for truth.
He will not fail nor be discouraged,
Till He has established justice in the earth,
And the coastlands shall wait for His law.'

(Isaiah 42:1–4)

Jesus was elected by His Father to bring justice to the earth,
for the non-Jewish nations as well as the Jewish people. It is
recorded twice, *'He will bring forth justice'* and a third time it
is stated, *'He will establish justice in the earth'*. That part of His
commissioning needs the fierceness of the Lion – Jesus is
likened to the King of the jungle, known for His strength and
power. He will come against the demonic forces, fighting
injustice to bring forth justice, whether He speaks to injustice
bound up in a person in sickness[6] or in an organisation that

---

[6] See Matthew 17:18

systematically abuses the vulnerable.[7] Jesus will show His mighty strength. We too are called to be as bold as lions in our call to fight against injustice, yet, we must also follow Jesus' call to be like Him in character in being 'gentle and lowly',

He will not cry out, nor raise His voice,
Nor cause His voice to be heard in the street.

(Isaiah 42:2)

This, in part, refers to Jesus' death on our behalf. Jesus said He could ask the Father for over twelve legions of angels and God would send them.[8] One legion, by the way, was a group within the Roman army consisting of between 3,000 and 6,000 soldiers – more than twelve times that amount were ready and willing to fight on Jesus' behalf, but Jesus chose not to operate under His rights, but under grace. I love the playfulness of Jesus revealed even in the garden of Gethsemane, after suffering such emotional turmoil at the knowledge of the suffering He was about to endure, and having released His life to His Father's plans:

Along come the soldiers to arrest Him.

'Whom do you seek?' Jesus asks.

'Jesus of Nazareth' they reply.

'I am He' Jesus responds.

His words are so powerful; the soldiers all fall to the ground! Did Jesus smile to Himself as He repeated the question to the baffled and dishevelled soldiers lying on the ground, 'Whom do you seek?'[9] As they led Jesus away, they knew without a doubt that Someone far mightier than they was *allowing* them to take Him!

---

7   See Matthew 15:3–9

8   See Matthew 26:53

9   John 18:4–8

This is the first lesson Jesus would have us to learn – to be gentle towards our attackers, and humble ourselves in situations that God would have us go through, either for the benefit of our own growth or the benefit of others. It is no good fighting against 'attacks' if it's in God's plan – for if we do, we then fight against God! The incredible part of Jesus' command that I could not comprehend for over 20 years is at the end of the sentence:

'Learn from Me for I am gentle and lowly, and *you will find rest for your soul.*'

If in the midst of attack, you can learn from Jesus to be gentle and humble, you will find rest for your soul – no matter what is happening to you on the outside, you will be in a place of rest – a place of peace on the inside. This I believe is a lifetime lesson. We must continuously learn from the Master – each incident may well hurt in itself – rejection, ridicule, and criticism all wound the soul and spirit, and some people are even physically beaten for their faith. In that moment, we have a choice to make – do we retaliate in the flesh; our mind, emotions and will taking charge, or do we bring it all before the Master, placing our wounds in His, for it was for this reason He went before us, to carry our sorrows.[10] If we will choose the latter, we will learn a little more from the Master, resulting in His beautiful promise – rest in our souls, Alleluia!

Secondly, Jesus would have us to learn to be gentle and humble in our every relationship. Some people are kind to their families and cruel to their colleagues or subordinates, others are kind to everyone but their family, taking out every vengeance for the day's mistreatment on them. Some will be

---

[10] See Isaiah 52:4

'lovely' to most, and brutish toward a few. None of these ways is acceptable to the Master!

> A bruised reed He will not break,
> And smoking flax He will not quench;
> He will bring forth justice for truth.

> (Isaiah 42:3)

Jesus never honoured one person above another. He demanded everyone be treated equally and reminds us we cannot hide behind title or pedigree in the day of judgement.[11] I love the fact that the more broken we are, the more sure we can be of getting a good reception from Jesus – He loves us in our brokenness and promises to restore us. In the Body of Christ, we so easily 'kick a man when he's down', but Jesus gets down there on the ground amidst all the dust and, looking us in the eye, says, 'Where are those accusers of yours? Has no one condemned you? – Neither do I condemn you; go and sin no more.'[12] **The devil condemns yet Jesus convicts! Condemnation keeps us locked in a cycle of sin, which leads to death; conviction of the Holy Spirit releases us from sin into fullness of life in Jesus Christ.**

Finally,

> [Jesus] will not fail nor be discouraged,
> Till He has established justice in the earth,
> And the coastlands shall wait for His law.

> (Isaiah 42:4)

In learning from Jesus, we will learn how to be gentle towards ourselves. Jesus never allowed discouragement to rule His life.

---

[11] See Luke 16:19–31; 18:9–14
[12] John 8:10, 11

When you've let God down through disobedience and rebellion, be quick to repent. Then leave it at the cross – condemnation is not your portion, forgiveness through Jesus Christ is your portion! It takes humility to admit your failing, but it also takes humility *not* to pick up the guilt at the end of your discourse with God! Christ has paid the price, so you don't have to! In accepting Jesus' gentleness and meekness towards you in that situation you will be rewarded greatly, for you will find rest for your soul!

The person called to be your greatest encourager after the Spirit of God is you! Living in Jesus, and allowing Jesus to live in you, discouragement will not overcome you, but you will overcome discouragement. Other people can encourage you, but only you live within the little home God has built – for you and Him alone to dwell. Your attitude alone determines whether you fail because of discouragement; do you believe circumstances and people's opinions or do you choose to believe God? David encouraged himself, commanding his soul,

'Why are you cast down, O my soul?
And why are you disquieted within me?
Hope in God, for I shall yet praise Him
For the help of His countenance.'

(Psalm 42:5)

Jesus continually humbled Himself before the Father, proclaiming,

' . . . the Son can do nothing of Himself, but what He sees the Father do; for whatever He does, the Son also does in like manner . . . I speak what I have seen with My Father.'

(John 5:19a; 8:38a)

Jesus knew He was nothing without the Father! When discouragement attacked, such as the news of the beheading of John the Baptist, Jesus sought the company of His Daddy, for in His presence, encouragement would be greater than any discouragement Satan can stir up.[13] When discouragement comes your way, be quick to follow Jesus' example! Get in the boat and sail away from the crowd, then turn to your God and lay down your heavy burden – release it all, and the Lord Jesus Himself guarantees *'you will find rest for your soul'*! Even in my formative years, before much-needed healing, I was blessed with an urgency within my spirit to bring every discouraging incident to my Lord; Jesus never let me down, always encouraging and filling me with His peace – thank God for His love and kindness!☺

---

[13] See Matthew 14:13, 23

4. Your Healing Shall Spring-forth Speedily

Five days after our entrance into the Novitiate, 'the whole world' as my Momma put it, joined together to raise money for Africa through Sport Aid. My brother John ran the six miles set, while Yvonne and I with four 'middlies' (my nick-name for the few middle-aged Sisters in the Congregation who 'ran the show') would join the local sponsored walk. Making a poster asking for donations, I took the simple idea of matchstick people from the Good News Bible, drawing four nuns with veils blowing in the wind, the leading two waving victory flags as they climbed the hills to reach the finishing line and two following prayerfully, while the two without veils twirled and jumped about excitedly. The retired Sisters couldn't participate in the walk, but being of missionary background, gladly gave donations out of their pocket money. Outings were so rare that having the opportunity to socialise on a day out with people other than nuns was such a treat!

A short time later, Fr. McKieran's new assistant, Fr. Watson came to visit from Chester. He and Yvonne immediately hit it off, having the same quick wit. As he was about to leave, Olive Oil decided to take a stab at humour.

'I was just thinking; being Fr. McKieran's assistant, that make you his ass?'

Fr. Watson gazed at her with unbelief before dryly answering, 'No!'

Yvonne and I held our breath in order not to burst out laughing. After his visit, Yvonne and I ran up to her room and began to howl with laughter. As our laughter became uncontrollable, I knelt on the floor banging the bed with the palm of my hands. How could she think Fr. Watson would find her suggestion funny? So engrossed in our laughter, we hardly heard the knock on the door before Olive Oil dived in –

'Novices are not allowed in each other's rooms!'

What?

'Sister Mary Kaitlyn, out of this room, and don't let me see you in here again.'

I glanced over at Yvonne in unbelief as I was marched to my own room.[1]

Yvonne recovered quicker than I, calling out, 'Sister Mary Kaitlyn, we've got free time now – would you like to go for a bike ride?'

I didn't dare look back; I could feel the eyes of fire glaring into my back. With a hidden smile, I called back as calmly as I could, 'Yes, ok then!'

O.O marched into the chapel while Yvonne and I quickly changed into the 'would like, but can't insist' forbidden tracksuits.

As soon as we took the bikes from the Rose Garden, we took the circuit we had walked numerous times with the 'the middlies'. Descending the hill of the main road for only a few minutes, we were soon winding our way along gorgeous

---

[1] **Footnote of Fairness:** 'Sr. Peter' ran the Novitiate in the way she thought best. She was not a bad person in that position, just rather 'pre-Vatican 2' (1962) (Sister Representative)

country lanes, farms and fields on either side with cows mooing, sheep bleating and dogs barking. The two of us behaved as if we were on 'Tour-de-France', racing recklessly around the bends. Sharing the characteristic of determination (or you may call it a 'stubborn streak'), neither of us would give up as we raced up the steep hill to the old church where the family at Brighton Hall worshipped in days gone by. Once there, we had a short distance before turning into the drive. The Hall looked as majestic as ever as we raced towards the finish – the Rose Garden was only seconds away! As we reached the bend, I was slightly in front. Wanting to avoid a collision, I looked back to see Yvonne's position as I attempted to miss the puddle-filled pothole to my left. Taking a wide berth, the bike wheels lifted from the ground, my body becoming parallel with the ground. No concern reached my head or heart; Evel Knievel had nothing on me; once around the bend, the bike would return to its vertical position and I'd win the race! What can I say! In my excitement, I perhaps forgot the power of gravity! Bang! Splash! I fell headfirst into the puddle! Jumping up from my embarrassment, wet and wounded, I resisted Yvonne's suggestion I should visit the infirmary in the main house for the nurse, Sister Henrietta, to examine me.

'No, I'm fine; I just need to get out of these wet clothes and have a shower.'

We never sneaked into the Novitiate as quietly as we did that day! Yvonne offered help, but no, I'd be okay. She sat outside the bathroom waiting – knowing! I managed to take off my wet clothes and shower, but could not use my arm to dress myself. Yvonne helped and escorted me to the Infirmary.

'Wounded Soldier', she announced to Sister Henrietta coming out of the dispensary.

Taking me into the treatment room, Sister Henrietta laughed, 'We had a blow-by-blow account of your accident.'

Sister Winifred, one of the patients, sat by the window while many others visited the land of nod.

'Two boys, cum – coming down the drive, cum – one fell off, cum – fell in that puddle, cum!'

Sister Henrietta had peered out the window, stretching her neck as far as she could to see, but the drive appeared empty. Concerned for 'the injured boy', she then went down to the main entrance and walked around to the side door, but saw nothing, returning to the Infirmary mystery unsolved.

Without a doubt, my right arm was broken. While Sister Celia, the Sister-in-charge, quickly prepared to take me to hospital, she announced, 'I'll ring over and tell Sister.'

Not wanting the fuss of a 'clucking hen', a quick anxious glance in the direction of Yvonne brought the desired response, 'No, it's okay, Sister. I'm going over now; I'll tell her what happened.'

As we headed to the city, filled with guilt and shame at my foolishness, I apologised profusely. 'It's not your fault – you can't help accidents happening.'

As far as character types go, Sister Celia and I could not be further apart. She and Yvonne always related very well – both analytical, they related through the mind, while I related primarily through the heart. I generally felt rejected by her because of my emotions, but in our visit to the hospital, Sister Celia could not have taken better care of me. Of course, I wasn't being emotional, so that probably helped! When checked-over, not only did my arm need to be put in plaster, but skin hanging off above my lip needed stitches. The whole right side of my face, swollen to impersonate the elephant man, was covered in cuts ingrained with gravel, the removal of which by a young nurse and a pair of tweezers left me truly nauseated!

Tired after our long drive and hospital visit, I longed for my bed, but Olive Oil wanted every last detail of my fall and treatment. I dramatised my tiredness in answering slowly and deliberately, with eyes drooping, but the Queen of Implication did not take the hint! I gave all the details before being allowed to go to bed. As I climbed the stairs, I cringed on hearing O.O call after me, 'Are you able to undress or do you need my help?'

'No, I'll be fine thanks!' (*'Why can't she just let Yvonne help me??'*)

Only two months earlier, I had been confined to bed with chicken pox. Regardless of a broken right arm, I was determined that I should not 'slack' for one minute, continuing my work in the main house and my responsibilities in the Novitiate. Our work in the main-house changed every few months and by this time, I was 'sacristan', taking care of the chapel. Olive Oil offered to free me from the responsibility, but I insisted I could manage. Of all the jobs I could have been doing in the convent, this was probably the most suitable for a 'one-armed bandit' – helping in the kitchen and infirmary, for example, definitely needed two arms. Duties as sacristan included keeping the chapel clean as well as the most important work of preparing the altar. Before I broke my arm, I competitively worked at reaching the fastest time to complete my responsibilities. The prize was having free time before lessons to go 'a-wandering' into other departments within the convent to socialise. The kitchen was usually my first port of call, the hub of the outfit, where there was always plenty going on. The aroma of scones, biscuits or cake for afternoon tea signalled 'perfect timing' for me to visit; the warm treats just out of the oven sitting on a cooling rack inviting me to take a bite!

I was determined my chores should take no longer simply because one of my arms was unable to help. As part of my routine in clearing the altar after mass, I collected two gigantic candelabra set on either side of the large table, carrying them to the sacristy at the back of the chapel. When I carried one in each hand some of the Sisters were impressed with my strength, but now, determined not to take a moment longer to complete my routine, I carried the two candelabra in one hand. On the first morning I attempted this feat, I was surprised to see a number of Sisters slip to their knees and with a look of anxiety begin to pray. I was soon joined by Sister Alison in the sacristy who requested I discontinue my 'antics' on account of Sister Marian's nervous condition, causing her to fall to the ground and shake profusely at sudden loud noises. I refused to change my plans, assuring Sister Alison I would not drop even a candle. She, of course, was not happy with my answer, and for the remaining weeks my right arm was inoperative, the Sisters present would continue to fall to their knees at the sight of me leaving the altar under such a heavy weight. Thank God, I never did drop anything, because although I stubbornly refused to change my plans, I would have felt absolutely terrible if I had been responsible for Sister Marian's 'attack of nerves'!

As many of the elderly Sisters in the congregation lived in Brighton, we celebrated many Golden Jubilees. This would be extra responsibility especially in the chapel, kitchen and dining room. On one such occasion, and me with only one arm, Yvonne offered to help me lay out the cassocks ready for the priests the following morning. As I opened one of the large cupboards, a black object flew out at me. I screamed 'Bat!' and ran, racing through the door into the chapel, firmly pressing my body against the large oak door, breathing a sigh of relief to be out. Mighty thumping shook the door while shouts began to get louder –

'Let me out of here!'

It was Yvonne; in my panic, I had locked her in the sacristy with a bat! Even to open the door to release her was a major demand to my emotions. As she continued banging and shouting, I sent messages to my tense body – *'move out of the way!'* After a few commands, I left the door and raced toward the chapel exit (just in case the bat should follow Yvonne). Yvonne looked as angry as Ollie would look Stan at in those old Laurel & Hardy movies after Stan would make some ridiculous blunder, and when Yvonne reached me, she gave me the same whack around the arm as Ollie would give too!

We ran to tell Sister Celia, sitting in her office directly opposite the chapel, of the unwelcome intruder. The obvious solution was in the hands of our 'rat catcher' – not that we had rats, but if we did, Sister Josephine would have been the person to catch them. Although not very tall, Sister Josephine was tough, built like a man and walked like a gunfighter in the old western movies. Being Tyrolese and 'of a certain generation' growing up on a farm, she was used to hard labour; consequently, no creature on earth frightened her. She was our woman! Although many of the older Sisters would be having a nap, Sister Josephine (known affectionately as 'Josepi') would still be working in the laundry or vegetable garden, so Yvonne and I were told to run and find her. We escorted Josepi to the chapel but did not go in with her, waiting in the office for her return.

Coming out with a carrier bag in hand, she waved toward the office. 'All finished.'

Sister Celia, with a look of horror, moved her gaze from the lifeless bag to Josepi's face. 'What do you have in there?'

'Vwat you zink? De dead bat!'

'But you're not allowed to kill bats!' Sister Celia answered anxiously. 'They're endangered species.'

Josepi clicked her tongue and blinked her two eyes, as she always did when she had the solution. 'No one vwill know – I vwill bury in de vegetable garden.'

As well as having celebrations in Brighton, there would be celebrations to which we would also be invited around the country. Only a few weeks after my bike accident, we were invited to the Mother-House in Chester. My scabby face was 'a sight for sore eyes' for the Sisters who lived with me, but my pride could not handle all the Sisters in Chester seeing me like that, so on the afternoon before our trip I spent my free time before the mirror in the bathroom, peeling off each and every scab. Thank God, they must have been close to ready to come off, my pride not leaving me with scars for the rest of my life! I was just, let's say, a little pink for a few days!

My broken arm was, for the most time, not too painful and the usual irritating itching overcome with a long knitting needle. I faced life without the use of my right arm as a challenge. By the time I was to have the cast removed, although I was not ambidextrous in the true sense of the word, I had learnt to write in calligraphy-style with my left hand. Yvonne and I would take turns in decoratively writing out the order of service for morning and night prayers, and as the weeks passed, I became more impressed; recognising the writing with my left hand was prettier than that done in previous weeks by my right hand. In my free time on a warm afternoon, I would still change into my green tracksuit and head to the bike shed. I didn't leave the grounds as I didn't want to face the hills but cycling with one arm on the flat was easy. Sister Finnian, on seeing me cycling the grounds one afternoon, commented on the fact that my escapades were a challenge to the Sisters' prayer life –

'You certainly keep us busy – no novice has ever needed as much prayer as you!☺'

When the cast was removed I had no problems with my arm, yet the wound above my lip would occasionally inflate like a balloon and cause terrible pain. I visited the doctor who explained I had what was called *'exuberant healing'*; my body, eager to heal, sent extra healing resources to the wound, but eventually, the doctor assured me, all would calm down.

On my return to the Novitiate, Olive Oil laughed at this title. 'That fits your character perfectly.'

I couldn't tell whether she was being critical or simply enjoying the recognisable parallel. Although she gave the impression of disdaining my exuberant character when I first entered the Novitiate, I had tapered it enough for it now to be acceptable.

We were in the height of summer and I could embrace life with two arms. In the summer months, I had occasional family visitors, always chauffeured by the only driver in the clan, my brother Chris. One evening he left just before Evening Prayers, after a nice visit with our sister, Norah, and her family. As our Evening Prayers turned to personal requests, I had the uncanny sense an accident was about to befall my family on their journey home and I should ask God's protection. Chris later argued with tongue in cheek that God did not answer my prayer, as swerving to miss an out-of-control car, Chris landed in a field, needing to be towed out by the farmer's tractor. Yet, we both knew God saved my family from personal harm.

Another important day out on the convent calendar was a day up in Chester for the annual Garden Party. Only two hours from my home, this was a perfect place for my family to meet up with me. I, of course, was given a job to do, but still I managed to have quality time with my family, and they had plenty to keep them entertained in all that was going on. My younger sister, Patricia, had her precious little daughter with her – sixteen month old Marie-Therese, named so by me. Patricia had allowed me to name her little girl as she had felt that God had asked her to be a nun, a call she never answered. Feeling I was taking her place, and as a thank you to someone who would never bear children herself, Pat gave me permission to name her little bundle of joy. Years later when 'Marie' (pronounced Marry) changed her name to 'Marie' with the usual pronunciation, her mother presumed I'd be upset, but indeed I changed my own name while in the novitiate, so how could I be upset?

Sister Aiden, someone I wanted to emulate, managed to seamlessly merge her respect for authority and her Irish identity as a rebel. From the moment I arrived at Brighton as a postulant she always called me 'Sister', but when I officially entered the Novitiate, Olive Oil announcing I was no longer to be called 'Kaitlyn' but Sister Mary Kaitlyn, Sister Aiden renamed me 'Katey'. In a world where I was constantly corrected for calling people by their first name without their title 'Sister', I gratefully embraced my new title-free name. Signing my mail 'Katey' created a comfortable division between the life of obedience I had committed to and the freedom I dreamt of. Initially, I gave new people I met the choice to 'call me either Kaitlyn or Katey'. Within two years, however, no choice was given – **my name is Katey!**

Days like the Garden Party were rare and for the most part, Yvonne and I struggled with what seemed to us to be Olive Oil's pettiness, and those 'ridiculous implications' that, without an interpreter, we were unable to read! Wimbledon fortnight came, and Olive Oil went home to her sister's to spend day and night in front of the television – watching the rain and repeat matches from years gone by, for the most part! On leaving, she instructed us on what subjects to study, wanting written proof on her return. *'Do it in your own time'* she added. Arriving back at 2.30p.m., the usual time of our afternoon lesson, Olive Oil and I greeted one another in the kitchen as I was busy hand-washing my clothes. The next morning as our 'homework' was handed over I was asked why I was washing my clothes the day before when I should have been studying.

'But you said to do the work in our own time!'

'Yes, in your own time – your own time during lesson times!'

Yvonne and I, constantly 'at a loss with her', at least had one another; together we could get through this! I considered it a bonus that for a whole month, I had not had any sickness or accident and obviously, Olive Oil felt the same, commenting one morning we could now seriously become a Novitiate.

'It seems to me we've been more like an infirmary than a Novitiate!'

What she didn't know was Yvonne, hitherto a healthy sporty person, was not 'feeling so good'. Confiding in Sister Celia, the 'Superior' agreed Yvonne needed to see a doctor, but first she must tell the Novice-Mistress. An appointment was duly arranged with the doctor who diagnosed the root of her problems as 'stones' which needed to be removed surgically. While Yvonne waited for the date of her operation, she became weaker; no more cycling or jogging, she quietly held-on for the day she'd be released from her pain.

An even more exhausted person re-entered the Novitiate after her operation, and while all Yvonne wanted to do was sleep, she was put through the same ordeal as I had suffered only months earlier – she must, during our evening meal, give Olive Oil a moment-by-moment account of her time in hospital. Our evening meal ('supper') in the Novitiate was laid out in the dining room. We would collect our own choice of food on a tray and sit in the community room, returning for seconds as we pleased. Olive Oil, noticing Yvonne's plate was empty, offered to collect more food for her. Yvonne, naturally independent, replied she could manage. Olive Oil's demeanour instantly changed, looking highly offended before marching out of the room. Clattering of plates could be heard as she released her fury on the washing-up bowl.

'What did I do?' Yvonne asked, truly bewildered by Olive Oil's sudden change of behaviour.

'She wants to "nurse" you back to health', I replied.

Greatly discouraged, Yvonne answered, 'You'll make a great nun; you understand people.'

'So will you', I pleaded anxiously, as one pleads with someone who seems to be about to give up on life.

Yvonne shook her head, hopelessly. Handing me her plate, she instructed, 'Tell O.O I was tired and I've gone to bed.'

During Yvonne's recuperation, the Novitiate became a quiet, sombre place. For three months, I had behaved myself as instructed (in front of O.O anyway☺), sitting quietly during lessons and meals in the Novitiate, speaking only when spoken to. Yvonne, with little energy, hardly spoke at all. Olive Oil, after one of our lessons, asked me to remain behind. She had come up with what she considered the perfect solution – I was to become 'loud' again, telling funny stories that laughter may ring through the Novitiate once more. I followed her command and for two evenings, anyone listening at the window would have thought I was performing 'stand-up comedy'!

On the third day I returned to O.O, 'Sister, I don't want to be "loud" any more. It's not me!'

'No, it's marvellous. Why, Sister Stevie was just saying how wonderful it is to hear laughter in the Novitiate again!'

'But Sister, it's not "the real me" – it's a performance.'

'You're doing a great job – keep it up!'

And with that, I was dismissed.

Joyful Memories...

Party Games

The Sisters and my Momma celebrate my birthday in the 'Volunteers' year'

Ladies and the Tramp

Sisters' performance at the Centenary celebrations in 'Brighton Hall'

5. A Time to Gain, a Time to Lose!

For three days, Yvonne was 'an absolute pain' to live with; no one could do anything right! Coming out of the Novitiate together after breakfast on the first morning, without registering my own actions, I wiped my feet on the mat sitting outside the door.

Turning back to me, Yvonne scowled, 'I wish you'd stop doing that!'

'What?'

'You wipe your feet every time you come out of the Novitiate.'

I looked back at the mat, truly surprised. Laughing, I replied, 'I never noticed – rubbing off all the 'scum' I picked up!'

'And how you can share at breakfast those dreams you have is beyond me –they're all so obviously about being imprisoned in the Novitiate!'

'O.O always seems intrigued – she doesn't click-on.'

'She couldn't work out a jigsaw puzzle designed for a five year old!'

Changing the subject in the hope of cheering Yvonne up, I told her I had written a new sketch to entertain the Sisters, suggesting we practise it after lunch.

'You and your stupid plays – don't you know there are more important things in life.'

(Okay! Time to be quiet! I can't win!)

On the third evening I found out the reason behind Yvonne's bad mood, and the news turned my mood into rage!!! Yvonne, who never regained full health after her operation, did not feel able to remain in the Novitiate. She made her final decision the day before her first outburst, and had to bear the brunt of her parents' disappointment, all without telling me, as the powers that be didn't want me to be unsettled. I was so furious! Before you read on, let me prepare you – what I wrote in my journal will be too much for some – how could I be so irreverent, you cry! I only know God's grace allowed me to be so expressive, and because He reads our hearts, in the midst of shouting out 'hate', He knew I still loved Him and was, in my immaturity, finding a way to express my pain and fear:

Let me tell You, God – I HATE YOU! You, who brought me to this horrible Novitiate where I didn't want to be, but at least I had the consolation of Yvonne. What do you do? Take her away! I hate You! Why? WHY? WHY?

Why, Jesus, why must I be left alone? I shouldn't even be a novice, never mind the one-and-only novice! I can't believe You've done this to me! Why do You play with people's lives like that? It's so hard to come – and poor ol' Yvonne's had to leave.

*And that stupid Olive Oil! After Yvonne told me, O.O spoke to me about Yvonne leaving, telling me she thinks I have a vocation, but she'll let me know if she changes her mind! Who does she think she is? – God!?! Isn't our vocation our chosen life – chosen by God! When I'm not behaving as she thinks I ought, I haven't got a vocation! Stupid woman! She should say I'm not **responding to my vocation** as she* *thinks I should. Our moods are not a sign of whether we have the same vocation as we had last week. Lord, I hate her! She's lovely enough, and I'm sure, You being unbiased, can love her – I leave You to it! But she's going to have me under her thumb. I'm all on my own. I don't want to be moulded into a copy of her*[1] *. . . Don't expect me to survive much longer; she can only wash the floor with me so many times! I can't take it! From tomorrow, I'm all alone. Jesus, I just can't cope!*

Why, God, why, WHY, WHY???

Tomorrow came all too soon, and before lunch, Yvonne's parents arrived to take her home. We had our last meal together – worse than a funeral! At least, Olive Oil didn't sit at our table; the situation was uncomfortable enough! Sister Celia sat at the top of the table, Yvonne sitting between her parents on one side of the table, with me facing Yvonne with elderly Sisters on either side. If we were on retreat under the rule, 'no talking', our table would not have been as quiet as on that dismal day! Dishes of meat, potatoes and vegetables were politely passed around. I felt so incredibly sick; all my emotions seemed to be in my throat! I could not believe I was being made to sit and eat! I placed five garden peas on my plate, and after twenty minutes had managed to eat two of them!

Celia laughed at the sight. 'You won't get full on that!'

'I'm already full!' I mumbled into the plate.

The table returned to awkward silence. I knew when this meal was over Yvonne would be taken from me, and it took

[1] **Footnote of Fairness:** Much of 'Sr. Peter's' emphasis as Novice Mistress was on 'character forming', as it would have been before the reforms of Vatican 2 (1962). This may have seemed controlling to a young woman in the 80s. (Sister Representative)

all my will power to sit through pudding without crying! After the car sped up the drive, I ran – far from everyone – to the woods, weeping as I ran, and the further I got away from the Convent, the louder my weeping became! I hadn't been told I could have the afternoon off, but I was taking it – no way could I sit across from Olive Oil in a lesson – not today, maybe not ever! Alone in the woods, I could receive the comfort of my Jesus. Still, as I returned to the Novitiate, I couldn't imagine how I was going to cope without Yvonne! I had a confidante in Sister Caris, only a phone call away up in Chester, but I only turned to her when I really felt I could not cope. When things were merely *'painful'*, I could talk, shout, and even cry with Yvonne – whatever it took to release the pain. Now she was gone!

As I opened the front door of the Novitiate, Olive Oil came to greet me. I kept my head down, lifting only my eyes to acknowledge her, all the time moving toward my room. Of course, life still went on. I must meet Sister Stevie and Olive Oil in the chapel for prayers at 5p.m., and then sit through the evening meal with them! As soon as it was over, I retreated to my room.

Jesus, I can't face anyone. I can't look anyone in the eye. Eye-to-eye contact and I'll burst into tears! Sympathy and I'll scream! Lord, I'm just too emotional and so sensitive. And stupid Olive Oil is so pathetic, trying to make conversation – anything and nothing! I can't cope with her, and if she keeps giving me attention she won't be able to cope with me! Can't You shut her irrelevant chitchat up? Everyone else leaves me alone; why can't she? Everyone accepts I am upset and need time and space. She even says she thinks the same – so why doesn't she prove it and leave me alone! I need space to sort out my emotions. I can't

handle life if I don't know how I feel about it. Lord, I want
time to be me, to sort myself out and I want You to give it.
So, keep that wretched woman out of my hair!

Only the next day, Olive Oil frustrated me by what I saw as
her 'little' mentality in her little world. Taking down the
'liturgy list' temporarily, she returned it to its position with
Yvonne's name cut out.

Stupid woman, why didn't she take the whole list down?
So now, she's put the net curtain back up in the kitchen –
the day after Yvonne has left! We weren't novices very long,
probably in early June, when she took it down to wash. Both
Yvonne and I said we preferred it down, giving more light,
so she agreed to leave it down – and now, look! (Jesus, I feel
so pinned-in!) She's laying down the law again: 'You might
be the only novice, but you're not my equal; you are a
novice and I ain't gonna let you forget!'
And now, to my lesson (God Help Me!)

Within two days of Yvonne's departure I presented myself
to the community as *'happy'* and *'surprised at this joy'*, and
while I knew God's peace at certain periods of the day, 'happy'
and 'joyful' were exaggerations.

That is my downfall – pretending all is fine, while in all
honesty, physically, mentally, spiritually, and emotionally I
am still upset. I don't mind not being honest with others, but
with my own self I want to be true. I know if I follow the
path of pretence even I will become convinced for a week or
two – and then POW! I will go into a deep depression. I
would rather face the reality now while it is acceptable to be
sad. Lord Jesus, help me to be myself, even if it's only when

I'm alone with You. Show the real Katey to me, Jesus, and
grant me the gifts I need to persevere.

By the next day, I was even willing to assess my true feelings
toward Olive Oil!

Can I see the good in her, but don't want to acknowledge it
because I'm afraid of change, seeing it as a weakness? Am I
afraid to like her in case I begin to trust her? Can I ever trust
her? I'm sure if I looked deep inside my subconscious I'd find
I'm bitter toward her because of Yvonne's departure, but my
real anger and even **hate** *toward her comes from what she said*
to me on the day she was blunt about my behaviour – almost
5 months ago now! I don't mind what she said to me about me
– I needed to be corrected, but what about the things she said
about Sister Caris – are they true, Lord? Does Sister Caris find
me to be the problem Olive Oil says she does? Is it true she asks
many people's advice on how to cope with me? Am I really so
much trouble? Is there no love? Am I demanding too much,
and she as a Christian, rather than a friend, responding?

From the moment Olive Oil claimed the above to be true,
I not only never mentioned Sister Caris publicly, but whenever
she was mentioned, my face remained completely motionless
– there were plenty of Sisters abroad whom I had never met;
their names never got a response – neither would Sister Caris's
name!

My attempt not to mention Sister Caris in the Novitiate
one time went disastrously wrong! While all of Brighton Hall
waited eagerly to hear if Caris had received a new appointment, Sister Celia had spent the day with her but came back
without news. Discussing it at supper, Olive Oil, eager to
know, suggested I ring Sister Caris to find out. I refused,

internally vowing, *'I wouldn't tell you, even if I did!'* Later, however, my curiosity got the better of me and I rang Caris. My plan was to share the news of her appointment with Yvonne and 'have a giggle', observing quietly to see how long the other Sisters needed to wait before news filtered through to the country, but Sister Caris ended the call with, 'Be sure to give the information to the right people first.'

Little could she know what an awkward position I was putting myself in agreeing to such a request; how could I give a message from a person I pretended never existed, especially to the one whom I considered the arch enemy of our friendship! I cringed as I told Yvonne, 'I've promised her I'll tell Olive Oil, but I can't!'

Yvonne brewed up a cunning plan – she would walk over with Sister Stevie from the main-house, telling her the news on the way. Without a doubt, Stevie would bring up the subject at supper. Sure enough, Yvonne's plan worked like clockwork! Yvonne and I smiled at one another as at supper, Sr. Stevie began to inform Olive Oil, 'Have you heard, Sister?'

The whole story out, Olive Oil's head immediately spun 180 degrees toward me, her eyes piercing into my soul. 'Did you know?'

My face turned bright red as I looked down to my plate and stuttered, 'Y-e-e-e-e-s', before picking up my tray and running out of the living room to cool down and regain my breath. Yvonne was left stunned and disappointed by my bad performance, and I had to accept I would not be winning any Emmy Awards for my performance!

Now, in my position as the 'lone novice' I must face a problem I hadn't considered encountering in my plan to pretend Sister Caris didn't exist – Olive Oil informed me of her visit – *tomorrow*! What if I had to sit with her and Olive Oil; how would I cope, and what expression was I supposed to display? Then Caris was giving Olive Oil a lift to London as O.O was to attend a weekend of training in 'Spiritual Formation' (how to train young men and women as priests, monks and nuns). I knew I would be discussed! Fearful that Sister Caris would take Olive Oil's side against me and therefore reject me, I decided to reject her first:

I trust neither party! I never want to trust Sister Caris
again with my emotions. (She'd be the happy one if I kept to
that resolution!)

My concern about sitting with them proved unnecessary; no sooner had Caris arrived than she sped off with my Novice-Mistress beside her. I followed suit, disappearing from the convent on the bike, taking myself on a mystery tour; I just kept cycling. I encountered the usual farms, animals, and hills, as well as three lovely lakes. At the first lake stood an old mill with a gas pump close by – looking like a scene from the Walton's, I found it gorgeous. The most predominant memory of the journey, though, was the uphill struggles. For the last five miles, it seemed the hill was a continuous ascent without respite. I was tired and my bones were aching; I began to wonder if I was doing more harm than good, but I wouldn't stop; no hill was going to get the better of me! I asked myself why I couldn't be as determined in the life I had chosen. I was holding on. In not letting go, I showed determination, but I was no better than the spider I had seen in the downstairs bedroom, hanging from a web. Blowing in the wind, its hanging on was pointless because it was dead!

That's how I feel; my brain is dead! I'm moving from one
day to the next like a zombie. I want my brain to be active
again, but I feel my head has been crushed!

On the bike, I found the downhill journey a struggle too
– for a very different reason – responsibility!

*If I were to fall, I'd be in serious trouble with the Sisters. It's
not the easiest thing to live with forty-five complaining Sisters!
Holding onto the brakes caused great distress within, and at
those times, I had no desire to go on a bike ever again! I was
ready to curse the downhill slopes that only months ago
brought such exhilaration. Is this the life I must embrace –
must I restrain myself from doing things I love, things that give
me joy, because I'm now responsible for the Sisters' feelings?*

On Sunday, Sister Caris delivered the Novice-Mistress back
(oh, well!☹) Olive Oil asked Caris to talk with me, and on my
part, the resolution of two days earlier long forgotten, I also
wanted to chat with her – I needed to speak to someone who
I felt understood me! Olive Oil had conveyed the problem to
Caris – a lack of communication brought about by a lack of
trust on my part.

'*And I never want to trust her either, not even with the simplest
details of my likes and dislikes, let alone my emotions, my feelings!'*

Even my Momma had written after Yvonne left, sympathis-
ing with me for being left alone, but in a bid to settle me,
suggested,

*I think you should try and trust Sister Peter (the name by
which people usually called my Novice-Mistress☺) because
all the things she said to you would be trying you out, to see
what you're made of. If you trust her, you have a good
chance of winning.*

I couldn't explain to Sister Caris or my Momma that in
feeling so misunderstood by my Novice-Mistress about

simple things, I couldn't take the chance of trusting her, opening myself up to her on a deeper level in the hope she *might* understand and therefore accept me – the risk of further rejection was too great! Instead I shared with Caris all the negative feelings I had toward Olive Oil over Yvonne leaving, and how in missing Yvonne I sometimes expect her to come back – the child in me – *'But she ain't coming back and I have to carry on!'*

Sister Caris assured me I was using my determination to carry on. 'If only you could see', she said with a big smile, which in turn brought a smile to my face – she could see from outside. I couldn't!

The following day, the eve of my first anniversary of entering the congregation, I was so grateful to God for more visitors – Cath and Julia, who had been volunteers with me were given permission to visit for a couple of days. Sister Aiden, a much-needed support to me, had been away, and Mother Anastasia had brought her home. I was full of gratitude, but the most important time of the day was the opportunity to talk privately with Mother Anastasia – audience with the Pope or tea with the Queen simply could not compete! I found Olive Oil as straight as a country lane and treated her accordingly, but Mother Anastasia was 'real', as straight as a Roman road, putting me at ease to be honest with her. I'm told that in her care of children in the Rescue Society, the more difficult a child, the more compassionate was Mother Anastasia's response.

Certainly with the 'wayward novice', she spoke tenderly. 'What is the greatest problem for you – after missing Yvonne, of course?'

My candid answer fell easily from my lips, 'Trusting Olive Oil' (though, obviously, I didn't use that name☺). As I told her about the day I was 'put in my place', everything came spilling out. 'She said *you said* I was off the rails and needed to be brought into line.'

Mother Anastasia's right side of her upper lip rose as she tried to hide a smile. 'I didn't say that – I said you were rather lively and would need to calm down.'

I immediately told her what Olive Oil had said about Sister Caris – that she didn't care for me, how she didn't want anything to do with me but found me a great problem, and how this was the nucleus of my problem regarding trusting the Novice-Mistress.

This time there was no smile alongside Mother Anastasia's reaction. 'Sister Peter had no right to say such a thing to you. It is totally untrue! You must know that yourself, and you must reinforce your trust in Sister Caris.'

My eyes filling up with tears, I looked down and asked, 'Is that done through prayer?'

'Yes', Mother Anastasia answered, reaching to touch my arm and encourage my face to be lifted again, 'but first you must believe me!'

Later, I was able to share with Jesus,

I appreciated being able to speak to Mother Anastasia about my feelings without being condemned. Olive Oil made me feel so guilty for loving Sister Caris, but God's love is nothing to be ashamed of. (I would, however like to be able to say that with conviction!)

Mother Anastasia, a great advocate of prayer, believed my relationship with Olive Oil could be resolved through prayer – if I prayed blessing on her, God would change the situation. I too knew the power of prayer – knowing prayer could move mountains, I shared how sometimes I would pray for the Novice-Mistress and then stop, becoming fearful

– if the obstacle was removed, I might like her, even trust her!

Mother Anastasia answered dryly, 'At that point, start praying for yourself!'

Mother Anastasia's niece had taught me at school, and I found them to be very alike, especially their dry sense of humour. Some people looked positively afraid of Mother Anastasia when she 'joked' with them, but I just returned the compliment – and she seemed to enjoy the banter! When I told Mother Anastasia her brother had been like a father to me in the Charismatic Renewal, she replied, 'Oh, no, you're not trying to tell me we're related!'

Today, behind closed doors we could relate on a deeper level. Again comparing her to the Novice-Mistress, Olive Oil focussed on my negative characteristics, compounding my sense of failure. Mother Anastasia could be honest about my darker side while taking the time to illuminate my brighter qualities of compassion, creativity, and love. It was easy for anyone to see I was easily hurt because of sensitivity. Instead of simply telling me to 'toughen-up', Mother Anastasia suggested I make my characteristics work for good. Talking about my future, she encouraged, 'Use your sensitivity when you are in a place of leadership to make sure you don't hurt people – because you know how it feels.'

She did me a lot of good, Jesus, far beyond boosting my ego – I think she may have reached my soul because she sees my character in context. In her assessment of the good and bad in me, she concluded I am a lovely, loved and loving person. Thank You for her – and she tells me we both celebrate our entrance into the congregation tomorrow – see, we are related☺

6. Be Filled with the Spirit

Because I had friends visiting, I was allowed my anniversary day off – no work or studies. Two years previously, Cath, Julia and I began our voluntary year together, nervous at what lay ahead. We had experienced a great year together – not all easy or enjoyable, but together we had survived the lows and revelled in the highs. We had laughed our way through retreats as well as real treats, from spinning on the Waltzer at Blackpool when we first arrived to dancing the salsa in Spain before our year ended, as well as enjoying birthday parties at home and an end of year meal in the most luxurious hotel any of us had ever seen. We all were expected to work hard, and when it came to time off, we tended to go a little wild – kids again! One evening, Sisters Angelina and Marietta, in charge of us, went to the main convent and we like small kids, instead of the 'young ladies' we were supposed to be, decided to have a water balloon fight. Squeals of laughter amidst the ducking and diving, water splashing all over the place as balloons splattered on walls and carpets. Our fun carried on for two hours, running back and forth to the kitchen and bathroom sinks for refills. Claire, the youngest of us, and the most conscientious, recognised the time; the Sisters would soon be returning! Everyone to her station, quick! The balloons were collected, fallen cushions returned to their seats, towels laid out on carpets and stamped upon to soak up excess liquid and hair dryers positioned by every downstairs socket to dry out the wallpaper. If the Sisters knew of our escapade, Sister Marietta would be upset, but not say a word, but Sister Angelina – oh, no! No one ever wanted Sister Angelina to know what we had been up to; she knew how to scold you good and proper! Whoever put her in the position of keeping a group of youngsters in line knew what they were doing! Rozzi, our Scottish red-haired lyricist, who in quieter moments, led us in gentle worship, anxiously called from the lookout point in the darkened dining room, 'They're here!' Hairdryers were ripped out of the sockets and wet towels hidden behind the sofas as we all raced into the big sitting room, jumping into 'cosy positions' in front of the television, pretending we'd sat there all night.

Cath cheekily called out as the Sisters passed the open door, 'Have you had a nice night, Sisters?'

Peering into the living room while passing, they politely answered in the affirmative, before Sister Marietta asked, 'And have you had a nice night?'

'Quiet', Cath answered with a grin. 'Just watching the tele'!'

As they walked away, Cath kicked the door closed, and we all burst out laughing. The Sisters would have heard our secret laughter a lot – the source of our amusement was a secret, but our laughter was very public! Sister Angelina, in charge of the housekeeping and as strict as she was, was also naïve. I loved the thick crusts on the loaves of bread she bought. At night as we made our supper, if there were no crusts left on the loaves sitting out I would go to the freezer and take out the crusts from the loaves stored there.

One day, Sister Angelina announced, 'Do you know – the bakery sometimes forgets to put the crusts on the loaves?'

Everyone burst out laughing.

'No, honestly', she insisted, 'there's many a time I take out a loaf from the freezer and there are no crusts either side!'

This made us laugh all the harder and whenever we quietened, it only took a glance in one another's direction for eruptions to begin again.

Sister Angelina had lived in Kenya for over 40 years, consequently belonging to that culture more than the British culture she grew up in. God had told me the previous year I was to become a missionary in Africa, but Africa's a big continent! Sister Angelina's absolute love of Kenya birthed in me a heart for Kenya. I loved to spend time looking at photographs of Sister Angelina's life in Kenya, every photo inducing a story. With amazement in her eyes, she told of black babies being born 'white' before their true colour appeared. She spoke of individual girls, who against all the odds, went on to achieve great goals. She explained 'Hakuna Matata' long before *Lion King* reached the film studios – *'no worries'* was a way of life, people happy to sit and wait all day to be seen by doctors even if afterwards they had a five hour walk back home.

The very first time Angelina saw me clean the dining room, she delighted my soul as she exclaimed, 'You clean like a Kenyan – they remove all the furniture to clean the room too!'

I never really felt like I belonged in England, but, thanks to Sister Angelina's input, over a decade before I should arrive in Kenya I believed I belonged – what a gift! As a novice, I expected I would train initially with the Rescue Society as a Social Worker and later be sent out on mission to Kenya. My life was pretty much mapped out, I thought. Julia thought the same of her life. She had intended to join Mother Theresa's Sisters of Charity in India, training in Rome, but because she needed regular medication for thyroid problems, the Sisters could not take her. From believing she should join a very active order, Julia had now been led to go to the other extreme – a life of enclosed prayer in a Carmelite Monastery in the Peak District above Sheffield. Time has proven this to be God's leading as Julia remains there, content and shining for Jesus, to this day. Cath was in a period of transition, returning to her hometown, seeking work and a home, but most importantly, felt 'settled in herself'. I was later able to visit her in a home that she had made very beautiful.

'The girls' only came to visit for two nights and so, all too soon, it was time for them to leave. I was allowed to accompany them to the train station. Waving them off, Sister Maggie-May and I did a little bit of shopping before returning to the car. Maggie-May rummaged through her handbag, searching for keys as we entered the car park, but no keys appeared. Standing at the side of the car, she continued to look. As I came to the driver's side of the car to stand with her, something shiny, dangling from the steering wheel caught my eye. I looked closer.

'I found them!' I announced, pulling at the car door handle, but it was locked.

Maggie-May pulled at the handle. No movement! This was before the 'norm' of everyone carrying a mobile phone. We scanned the perimeter of the car park to see if a phone box was in view. Nothing! Maggie-May, needing to return to Brighton immediately to follow a tight schedule in caring for the retired and sick Sisters, clasped her face with her hand. With eyes half-uncovered she looked at me and said, 'Dear God! How's He going to get us out of dis mess?'

Two men entered the car park, passing us by to reach their own car. Maggie-May immediately accosted them, and with her high-pitched Cork accent begged, 'Please, yous just have to help us! I've locked de keys in de car and we don't know what to do!'

The older of the two men, in his thirties, did as we did – he tried to open the door. When that didn't work he leaned against the driver's door and peered through the window vertically, straight down into the body work. Looking up, he said to his young companion, in his 20s, 'Go get the wire.'

'You've got to be joking', the other replied.

'What they gonna do – they're a couple of nuns, and they need our help.'

Turning to Sister Maggie-May, 'Now, if we get your door open, you're not going to report us to the police, are you?'

'Of course not', Maggie-May answered.

'And you're not going to learn any bad habits from us, are you?' He laughed before continuing, 'We don't want to hear about any car thieves dressed as nuns.'

At this, Sister Maggie-May blushed.

'No, I didn't think so', he confidently answered, before turning to his friend. 'So, get the wire!'

The younger of the two went to their car and came back with what looked remarkably like an unravelled coat hanger, passing it to 'the boss', who in less than a second lowered it into the body of the door and chivalrously opened the door for Sister Maggie-May.

'There you go, Sister; Safe journey home!'

Amidst a thousand thanks, we loaded up the car and sped off in the direction of home.

'Well would you look at dat', Maggie-May marvelled. 'We asked God for help and if He didn't send us professionals!'

It was quite 'normal' for me not to communicate on the journeys to and from 'home', and the Sisters were all used to it by now. They misinterpreted my actions to mean I didn't like travelling, but on the contrary, I found travel therapeutic.

Looking out at the moving world, I would escape into my own thoughts, sometimes just appreciating the cascade of colour in the changing countryside or the ingenious cloud formation in the sky, other times I might dream of travelling to lands I hadn't yet seen. I might even imagine what it would be like to pop home, just for an hour, to share a hug with Mum, play with my nephews and nieces, and take my dog, Amigo, for a walk, accompanied as always by the family cat, Luke. Today, however, my thoughts were a little more sombre. A word I almost continuously accused myself with was *'failure'*. I had just had two friends to visit, and I failed to appreciate their visit, or attend to their emotional needs because I was full of self-pity for being left alone, the only novice. I failed to appreciate Olive Oil who allowed the visit, and instead criticised her to anyone who'd listen. Little did I know the next day Olive Oil would reiterate those feelings! In studying 'Perfectae Caritatis' (Latin for 'Perfect Charity') we looked at community living. Olive Oil pointed out that she could see in me a desire to be accepted. To be accepted, she advised, I must first accept others, and secondly, recognising my failure to accept others, begin to behave in an acceptable manner.

'I want the Novitiate and those within it to be respected. You should not breathe a word to anyone about our situation. If you want to moan, moan to the Lord!'

In a nutshell, I was no longer to speak about the Novice-Mistress! I didn't so much criticise her as mock her in mimicking, but as this would hardly stand up as good defence, I chose to remain quiet! In the few days she had been back from the 'Spiritual Formation' weekend she had mentioned on numerous occasions the one point she appeared to learn from the priest's teaching; 'the discontinuity of the young in their age of idealism'.

'As he said', she would insist, 'young people sing and speak of love, yet forget this has to be put into practice!'

Olive Oil informed me self-awareness and a humble spirit was needed if there was to be any hope of change in my behaviour.

'I know', I replied.

Unfortunately, we can all pick up the jargon, but all is theory! It's on the practical tests that we – I – fail. I KNOW I FAIL!

I seemed to have a week of bombardments in 'getting the message across'. In our constitution lesson, we reached the chapter on 'Novitiate' and one evening at supper, Sister Stevie inadvertently chose 'community' as her constitution to be discussed.

I see what you want me to learn, but I keep it all very theoretical. I have to accept the Novice-Mistress! Why is it so difficult? She's lovely enough and is very good to me. She's quite gentle and always makes nice conversation. Why am I holding on to my heart as if I'm clinging to a baby protecting him from his alcoholic father? Why can't I let go and let love be our communication? Jesus, I don't want to wait until I'm no longer a novice to get on with her. I couldn't be satisfied with that! It would all be false, simply acting; I want to love her now, Lord!

In prayers before bed, as I listened to Saint Paul's letter in which he spoke of running forward toward the goal instead of looking back, I decided to put my failures behind me and resolved to relate fairly towards Olive Oil. Unfortunately, before I even attempted to put this new resolution into action I aborted the plans as thoughts of the contradictions spilling out of her mouth flooded my mind. I questioned God:

> *Why did she say I was doing great just before Yvonne went into hospital in July, and then after Yvonne left tell me I've had a poor attitude since June? I don't mind her correcting me – that's her job, but I wish she wouldn't contradict herself. I can't relax because I expect her to jump on me any minute!*
>
> *Jesus, don't I say* **'If you knew me yesterday, don't think you automatically know me today'***? If I were willing to believe the same for others, I would accept Sister Peter for the joy she brings today instead of distrusting her because of the pain she brought yesterday. Lord, I have to live with her – and accepting her is the only way!*

A dramatic change that was about to take place in the Novitiate was that we were to go to Seminary College for some of our lessons. Mother Anastasia sensitively cancelled, what would have become, one-to-one lessons with the residing priest, suggesting it would be good for me to be around other young people (and hopefully cheer me up enough to cultivate a positive attitude back in the Novitiate)! Of course, the Novice-Mistress must accompany me to college, and as she didn't drive, Sister Alison needed to accompany us too. I was totally embarrassed by this, my every move monitored, judged and discussed. Even in the classroom I had my treasured journal with me and wrote,

> *'Won't you let me go home?' (My real home, that is, to my family in Yorkshire.)*

I then complained a little more about my precious Novice-Mistress who was standing outside the classroom annoying me by whispering with Sister Alison, before writing:

Jesus, You are going to work in me, aren't you? You are going to change me? You do the impossible, don't you? Jesus, You saw me share the sign of peace with her. I said I'd give the outward sign. I leave the inner healing to you. It's my only way forward, Lord. Jesus, please don't take too long!

In the coming week, I would experience days of peace that could not be accounted for; nothing had changed, I simply felt peace in my heart. This sense of peace was further strengthened when a Franciscan priest, Fr. Paul Hill, came to give a retreat. He had a docile expression of love for his Master, similar to the love my dog, Amigo, showed me whenever I returned home. Every communication was flamed with the Holy Spirit and his voice so peaceful. Enveloped in the Spirit of peace, one could float to bed in assurance at the end of the day of God's love. On one of the days, however, I missed out because we were at College, and duties in the evening meant I was late for the evening session. This was my night of discontentment! I chided myself,

This retreat will not go on forever. It doesn't matter how holy a person is or the amount of insight he might express, ultimately I can only turn to God for consolation and words of wisdom and love. But, I never know, Jesus – When will I feel Your consolation, when will I hear Your words of wisdom, when will Your love feel close to me? When will I be happy in You?

I loved studying the Bible so was excited to join Fr. McGough's Bible lecture the following Monday morning –

until he began that is! Studying Creation in Genesis chapter two, he named his lecture, *'Man should not be alone'*. Note-taking was not necessary; ready or not, this teaching was reaching my inner-being! Out came my little lilac 'Recollections' book for me to respond directly to my God:

I am alone, I am apart,
Belonging neither to horse nor cart.
I am alone, I have no friend.
To all their rules I cannot bend.

I am alone, I am distraught;
Angry with my every thought.
I cannot live this life my God;
I cannot give the approving nod.

My life no longer is my own.
'Man was not meant to be alone.'
Lord, I cannot trust, I have no faith.
I do not believe You're keeping me safe!

This structured life I cannot live –
To all these rules I cannot give.
Can't you hear my inward Groan –
My God, I do not want to be alone!

On our return journey to Brighton, my 'bodyguards' chatting incessantly in the front of the Convent car, I couldn't help but meditate on my strong feelings exposed in my poem and by bedtime had become totally disillusioned with the life I was trying to live. I wrote to my Jesus:

Considering a life of chastity, poverty and obedience
spark-off many problems. I will not live in obedience to

*Man, I cannot live this Order's poverty, and life-long
chastity would be a ridiculous hope! Christ, I don't want
to be alone! I am so alone! I want a companion. I want a
friend. I need to be loved. I don't know if I can love you like
a Religious should. I'd like a friend to call my own; I'd like a
love that is special. Man was not meant to be alone, and
within Community, I feel alone!*

I determined to leave within days. I would contact my
Momma, telling her I'm coming home, and ask her to arrange
for my brother Chris to collect me. I would avoid asking her
or Olive Oil's permission; the facts would be clear – *I'm leaving,
no need for dialogue!* Before I slept, however, Jesus put in my
heart the request I read the letter Paul wrote to the Ephesians.
He reminded me of the wonderful spiritual bank presented
to me through His sacrifice; I'm adopted, accepted, and
forgiven by God, He's even willing to fill me with His own
wisdom, if I'll take it! Speaking to me as one baptised in the
Holy Spirit, Ephesians 5:18 became the central theme in
Christ's persuasive argument. 'Be filled with the Spirit' speaks
of choosing to be continuously filled with Holy Spirit. If I
would follow this instruction, keep filling-up on Holy Spirit,
Jesus seemed to insist in my heart, Holy Spirit would enable
me to do that which I cannot do through my own power or
resolve. I went to sleep 'chewing over' the arguments for and
against leaving; my sense of hopelessness versus Jesus' encouragement; Holy Spirit's grace towards me would enable me to
succeed! I woke the next morning to a unique sense of contentment, singing as I regained consciousness, *'The only way
out is the only way in and it's You!'*

*Thank You for the wonderful work of the subconscious. I'm
happy to be alone because it's the beginning of my journey*

with You – alone with my God! Olive Oil said she felt it could only profit me to have lost Yvonne. She doesn't know how right she was for now I have no one to confide in or 'gossip' with.

As I roamed the countryside on the bike that afternoon, I was beyond contentment in being alone, expressing excitement in recognising I was **alone with my God**.

Your world is beautiful and there is nowhere I'd rather be than in the untampered countryside. You speak so clearly through nature. One seeks to be loved and to be happy in life. I've found You, Lord. Please, keep me!

7. The Silver-Haired Head Is a Crown of Glory

I missed Yvonne for many reasons, not least her natural flair in hairdressing. Receiving only £4 pocket money per month, out of which we must purchase everything from toiletries to stationery, and clothing to gifts, Yvonne, thankfully, had the foresight to arrive prepared with a hairdressing kit. After she cut my hair, she had a queue of middlies asking for the same treatment. On leaving, Yvonne presented me with the kit, but I could not claim to be as promising! In only a couple of years' time, I would present my life through 'the adventures of my hair' in a 'psycho-drama therapy' class. I began my story:

Born with long jet-black hair that my older sisters would 'dye for', it soon fell out and I was left with a murky brown thick mass upon my head. At the age of two, all dressed-up for a family photo, I decided to complete some last minute preparations while Mum dressed my baby sister. Taking the nail scissors sitting on the dresser, I began to cut my fringe – all the way across – not straight – all the way across, a second time – still not straight – cut again, and again, and again! By the time Mum found me, I had a little tuft on the top of my forehead. At the age of seven, I read of the boy who had rainbow-coloured hair. Everything he touched turned to rainbow. I am not sure his magical powers enticed me as much as his 'funky' hair colouring, asking Mum's permission for the same. In shock, she screamed, 'No you can't!'

As an adult, when I tried to fulfil this dream, the hairdresser asked, 'Where are the cameras – this has got to be a set-up!'

I had to accept I could only have two colours. Choosing purple and pink, I was offered red and blue that came out orange and green! The good news was the dye should wash out in three to four washes . . . six months later, the colour was fading!

At the age of eleven, I was mistaken by a five-year-old for that 'long haired lover from Liverpool', little Jimmy Osmond! Wanting to run from this 'accusation', I continuously bombarded my Momma to allow and pay for a perm. Arriving at 'Harry's', armed with a photograph of Farrah Fawcett sporting long bouncy hair, I believed my troubles were behind me, and only compliments (especially from boys) lay ahead! Unfortunately, Harry had more experience in short, back and sides than trendy looks. He quizzed over that photo, turning it every which way to figure out how he would transport that look onto my head, his efforts taking all afternoon. As darkness began to descend, Mum sent my brother to check I was okay. Chris fell off his bike laughing as a 'Shirley Temple' look-alike exited the barber's shop!

Not much later, the Bay City Rollers style affected the whole school and everyone had to wear a feathered look. My little sister, Trish, and I had long hair, the feathering beginning at the ears. I decided I could trim our hair, saving Mum some money. Following the style, I did a successful job of Patricia's hair, and cut my own hair at the front and sides. Not being able to complete the task, I explained the style to my brother Paddy and asked if he could cut the back for me.

'That's easy', says he, cutting the top layer of my hair in a straight line from ear to ear.

Amazingly, he believed he had done a good job! I, on the other hand, had to face the humiliation of being seen like that for two weeks as I waited for Mum to have enough money for me to visit the hairdressers'.

In the chair, waiting my turn, one old woman was talking about 'young ones today and their goings-on'. 'Take her for example', she said, pointing to me, 'look at the mess of her hair – they just don't care – they call it fashion!'

As good a job as I did on Trisha's hair two weeks previously, she decided she should have her hair cut professionally too. When I went to pay, however, I didn't have enough money and would have to go home, a half hour's walk, to collect more. In panic I pointed to Trish, somewhat hyperactive in her behaviour, all but swinging from the lampshades, telling the hairdresser, 'I'll leave her here; hold her hostage till I come back!'

The hairdresser looked at me incredulously. 'No, it's ok; you can take her with you!'

At fifteen, one Saturday, a committed punk friend decided to turn me into 'a punk'. Descending the stairs with torn clothes, clashing colours, a million pins, blackened eyes and lips, crowned with a green Mohican, I asked my Momma how I looked.

She replied (as only a mother could), 'You'd look beautiful whatever you do to yourself!'

In town, I was totally embarrassed by all the stares, quickly leaving that stage of my life well behind me!

By the time I began the 'volunteer year', I sported a new style every month, enjoying expressing myself through hairstyles.

Within that time, of course, I wore the pink spikes to tell Mother Anastasia I wanted to join the convent, and had my last fling with my blue hair wowing the Pope and every moped rider in Rome. Lastly, there was my attempt at cutting Yvonne's hair after she had done such a great job on mine. What can I say? None of the middlies would be queuing up for me to cut their locks, for by the time I was done, Yvonne had better chance of passing as a monk than a nun! But even worse was in store for me as, after Yvonne left, no one would attempt to cut the back of my hair; I had to set up two mirrors to reflect one another and trust I had the dexterity to complete the task. As a novice, I wore every part of the habit except the veil – that was for after profession, but sometimes I was willing to begin early!

I was moving in the right direction in beginning to appreciate both my calling and Novice-Mistress, but I still had a long way to go! Agreeing I was better off without another novice to complain to, I nonetheless spoke regularly to Yvonne on the phone, telling her everything that happened. The calls to Sister Caris, though, came to an abrupt stop; I would prove to everyone, myself included, that I did not need to depend on her support. Others may make New Year resolutions, but I continuously made resolutions throughout my Novitiate training, this time promising myself I would not contact her for four months to break any dependency. Besides, I had the retired Sisters to turn to in my hour of need! I remembered a recently professed Sister while visiting the Novitiate sharing her longing during Novitiate days to get away from the old Sisters, assuring me I would become content when I 'get out'. I said nothing audibly, but within I objected, *'but they're my saving grace!'* having built up many good relationships with the older Sisters. One proverb says,

The silver-haired head is a crown of glory,
If it is found in the way of righteousness.

(Proverbs 16:31)

Many of the elderly Sisters chose daily to walk the way of righteousness; understanding retirement was not the end of their work, but a change of focus, an opportunity to fulfil the desire that for many first drew them to Religious Life – to spend time in prayer. In a Working Order (teaching, caring, nursing, etc), life can get so busy between the years of Novitiate and Retirement. Those who embraced 'the call' of deeper prayer in those years of retirement, I believe, revealed a crown of glory.

I had always loved to spend time with Jesus in the great outdoors; in the Novitiate, it became essential to me, allowing no room for assessment of my development. As well as enjoying bike rides, I would spend plenty of time in the grounds. Heading out of the Novitiate, I would cut through the large, well-stocked vegetable garden. Josepi's old hens, running freely, seemed content in their ignorance – they'd soon be good for nothing except Penny's curry pot! (By the way, she alone could make an old bird taste as succulent as lamb!) Before hunting season, I'd pass a covey of pheasants merrily growing fatter, unaware that in a couple of weeks they wouldn't know what hit them! As a complimentary gift from the farmer next door, a handful of these colourful birds would provide a feast on our dining room tables! I'd often see Penny enjoying the sights and smells of growing vegetables, choosing her ingredients to accompany the meat of the day, but I had little interest – probably because I felt robbed as a teenager when Mum married Bob and we moved into his house with two gardens. The front garden hosted his prize flowers and the back garden his prize vegetables, but where was the lawn for Momma's prize daughter! I couldn't now complain; in Brighton, I had acres of lawn to enjoy! If I should walk the grounds on a pleasant morning, there would be a line of elderly Sisters heading toward the cemetery for their 'daily constitutional', but I would pass by in favour of the privacy of the woods. Away from prying eyes, I felt free to be, but with shorter days and blustery weather, I needed to move indoors.

Believing God was asking much more of my time in prayer, and not wanting to be observed over at the Novitiate, I decided one Sunday afternoon I'd spend three hours in the Main House chapel. Sister Cleo, the one and only Swiss Sister I knew, who like Anna spent hours in prayer,[1] was there at the sailing of this, my virgin-voyage.

After two hours, Sister Cleo, the size of a pepper-pot and as deaf as a doornail, bellowed across the silent chapel, 'You haven't had bad news, have you?'

'No', I replied, my face turning a bright tomato red as those present turned to look at me.

'That's okay, that's all I wanted to know', she shouted back.

Relationships with most of the retired Sisters were very important to me. As the only novice, I loved being the apple of their eye, but their outings to other convents unnerved me as they always returned telling me how they informed the Sisters about the gem of a novice they were privileged to have in Brighton. I loved all the affection they bestowed on me; I just wished they would keep their praises between us! Disaster loomed, I was sure, in other convents where I had been so highly praised – I could never live up to their high expectation and rejection would surely await me! If I could have locked up these dear old sweeties in the cellar on Jubilee days, I certainly would have!☺

---

[1] See Luke 2:36–38

I'm not suggesting all the elderly Sisters walked the way of Christ's righteousness – a few were so cross! Sister Marian was one of the unhappiest people I ever met. She was also the skinniest, eating barely enough food to keep a sparrow alive. A scowl upon her darkened brow, her colouring sallow from lack of vitamin D, and wearing the old-fashioned full black habit, draining any sign of life from her face, did not present a very appealing picture! The only time she communicated was to rebuke; eyes would flare as hissing darted viciously from her mouth. I used to wonder 'Is she angry because she's ugly or is she ugly because she's angry.' She did smile once – at me, the novice she generally considered worse than useless – and the smile definitely improved her looks! Her natural sister, Sister Anna, from the same stock and yet so completely different, shone with a beauty within and was always full of smiles, performing acts of kindness throughout the day, part of her very nature. Why such a contrast, I wondered!

With Yvonne now gone, certain relationships became even more important to me. On most days, I would meet Sister Aiden who would share a scripture she had chosen from Morning Prayers or Mass to meditate on. The best time to receive her insight seemed to be later in the day, having repeated it to herself all morning, and then slept on it after lunch (God even speaks to unbelievers in their sleep, you know, let alone those who choose to meditate on His goodness!) I too shared my insights with Sister Aiden, appreciating my own spirit getting a 'workout'. When I was first 'born from above'[2] as a teenager, I spent a lot of time reading the Bible up in my bedroom. I would be so excited when I received new revelation and would bound down the stairs to share with my Momma and sister. First, I would be told to be quiet while the

---

[2] John 3:3 NJB

soap they were watching finished, then after I shared my insight I'd be met by two bewildered faces wondering what all the fuss was about. In Sister Aiden, I had found a 'sounding board' for which I was so very grateful! This level of sharing led me to trust her in speaking about issues – in actual fact I only ever had one issue; my survival in the Novitiate! Sister Aiden, with eighteen years experience as Mother General, had a great deal of wisdom and understanding, and would help me to 'cope', always leading me to focus on why I was there – to follow my calling.

'You won't always be in the Novitiate', she assured me, 'When you're professed and have your own work, then you'll be happy. Just hold on!'

When I told my Momma the date of Sister Aiden's birthday, she wrote,

Is it not great we share the same birthday? I always knew that we had something special. I even let her share you for a little while☺

Another almost daily top-up I appreciated came from the gentle and affectionate Sister Dorcas. She loved Jesus so much! His love flowed out of her like liquid gold, sweet as honey. Although we never arranged a meeting, our divine appointments always took place on a bench. In the good weather, as I collected a convent bike to go for a ride, Sister Dorcas would be sitting praying or quietly singing in the Rose Garden while most elderly Sisters slept. Or if the weather was poor, she'd be coming out of Chapel as I'd turn up and we would sit on the bench facing the wide stairs leading up to the library. Whatever the start of our conversation, Sister Dorcas's answer always led us to look at one subject – the characteristics of Jesus – His beauty, His love, His kindness, His mercy. She assured me no matter the trial, Jesus was always enough to carry me through! I never verbally shared anything I was going through, but sometimes I wouldn't be able to hold back the tears – she knew that to be 'a bad day'; taking me in her arms, Dorcas's eyes would also fill up with tears as she would assure me even more that Jesus' love and grace is always enough. No matter my experience, talking with Dorcas lifted my spirit; I walked away with hope; God cares!☺ These two ladies could not have been more different – one an Irish, well-educated, born leader, the other a modest, Tyrolese lady who preferred to remain in the background, both so incredibly important to my daily living.

Another saving grace was the timing of my moving departments, heading toward the infirmary. Being a people's person, and especially loving the elderly (second only after children), I was looking forward to interacting, and knew I could wholeheartedly throw myself into my work, forgetting my woes (or O.O's) during working hours. As far back as I could remember I enjoyed the company of 'old folk'. My lasting memory of Britain's currency changing from pounds, shillings and pennies to pounds and pence was meeting two little old ladies in the shop, totally baffled by the coins within their purse. Even though I was only a small girl, we spread their coins out on the counter and I gave them a lesson in counting modern money. For that short encounter, the adult-child role was reversed and I found their vulnerability endearing, wanting only to bring them through to a place of security. Of course, I didn't have the words then to express those feelings, but as I joined my Momma, collecting food off the shelves, I gave her a big grin as she told me she was so proud of me for helping.

During my school years I had done voluntary work in an Old People's Home, and after school, my first job was with Age Concern, supporting the elderly in remaining in their own homes. This varied from helping with shopping to arranging home-decorating to giving personal care.

Mum, knowing my prudish attitude, objected when I went for the interview, 'You'll never be able to give an old man a bath!'

Yet, I did – I just switched off!

I became a volunteer with the Rescue Society to train in childcare, but on viewing my C.V. was assigned to the one home set aside for the elderly. I enjoyed the work and loved the people, especially the Sister-in-Charge, Sister Judy. Never have I met such a likeable 'fruitcake' in a position of authority! When I shared how I could juggle, she excitedly responded, 'Oh, teach me!'

She jumped from the table to find impromptu juggling balls – and picked up eggs from the egg basket!

'You've got to be joking – we'd have smashed eggs all over the place!'

Undeterred, she looked around excitedly for a 'safer' alternative and came up with tomatoes!

'OK', I said, amazed, knowing Sister Judy's choice revealed naivety as much as it did confidence. She could already play two-balls so we were off to a good start. We began throwing three-balls (or in this case, tomatoes) as a team – Splat! Splat! Splat! – All three landed at Sister Judy's feet. Laughing, unaffected, she reached across to the basketful of tomatoes and grabbed three more. On we went, improving all the time – 5, 7, 8, 10 catches before a fall. Sister Pat came into the kitchen, her jaw dropping all the way down to the tomatoes beneath our feet.

'What are you doing?'

Her despairing question transported Judy back from childish fun to responsibility. Turning to look at the clock behind her, she announced, 'Oh my goodness, it's time for tea!'

Turning to me, she directed, 'You get the tea and cakes ready. I'll go help the old dears get up.'

'What about this mess?' Sister Pat demanded.

Sister Judy, as easy going as ever, called back as she headed down the corridor, 'Make sure you don't slip on it.'

I put the kettle on and quickly wiped up our 'doings' from all over the kitchen floor. As I arrived in the sitting room with the tray of cakes, Sister Judy was in the middle of telling the 'old dears' about her juggling lesson, 'And here's my teacher.'

(Oh, Lord, don't let her ask for another lesson in here – because, honestly, with Sister Judy you never could tell! *What Katey Did Next* has nothing on the adventures of 'What Sister Judy did next'! On a whim, one year, she ran a marathon – no preparation, just a good idea! She survived, so she did the same the next year, and the next – all in her 60s! On hearing of her exploits, her doctor insisted she prepare her body for such a strain, so for two weeks before running the marathon she began taking a stroll around the block each evening, yet was never out of the house for longer than 20 minutes!)

This job in itself was a pleasure because of working with Sister Judy, but I wanted to be trained up in childcare. Asking permission to move, I often felt like the 'spare part' being sent from home to home in search of the need of another pair of hands; I worked in the nursery and every home bar one, as well as in schools and people's homes preparing deaf children for Communion. It was not easy to be moved from place to place – I wanted to be like all the other volunteers, having the stability of one position for the year, but in retrospect I see everyone was perfectly placed; each girl's personality and gifting complementing her placement. My personal calling in life is to work with many people in various settings, and so, even in my youth, I was learning to work in a multitude of situations alongside diverse personalities.

Now was my time for stability! As much as I struggled against settling into the Novitiate, I had no problem settling in the infirmary, enjoying helping care for the sick Sisters. However, I may have thought I was doing a better job than I was! Everyone able attended Mass; this meant bringing the Sisters down in the lift, one by one, either supporting them if they could walk, or pushing them in wheelchairs if they couldn't.

One morning I shouted down the corridor to Sister Gillian, 'I'll be with you in a minute to take you down.'

'Take me down', she complained to Sister Greta, 'and plonk me down!

As well as caring for Sisters in the infirmary during the morning, I had the responsibility of preparing ninety-four-year-old, four-foot-seven, Sister Lucy for bed at night. During the day Sister Lucy, almost totally blind, would be cared for by Sister Dorcas and would grasp any Sister who greeted her with both palms to bring them close, nose to nose to recognise them, and then give them the biggest smile, 'Oh, Sister, it's you!' before giving a tender kiss on the cheek.

Her affirmation lifted many a 'middly' from a heavy heart to continue their walk with a skip and a jump (more than figuratively, in Sister Celia's case!) Amazingly, this same little old, blind lady spotted toenails I dropped on the floor. As I would deliver the majority of them to the bin, she would reach down and pick up the few stragglers, complaining to herself, 'Young ones; they never do anything right!'

As I would come back into Sister Lucy's focus, she would give me a smile, and tell me what a good girl I was, before wishing me a good night's sleep! Closing the bedroom door, I would hear the private prayer of this precious little Sister; she had spent the day encouraging others and now it was time to express her own heart to God – 'Take me home, Jesus, take me home!'

8. Confess Your Sins to One Another

Vivid dreams were the 'norm' for me, but waking one morning from a sexually explicit dream shocked me. In the dream, a man 'came-on' to me. Initially, I responded, but then became fearful. The man suggested he improve the atmosphere and left the room to collect logs to make a fire. I meanwhile picked up blue sandals and looked for my escape route while alone. Waking up, I recognised immediately menstrual pains I experienced in those days before Jesus healed me. I understood instead of waking from the pain, I had placed it into a dream, but I questioned God, 'Am I here because I am afraid of relationships with men? Should I be here, Lord, or am I hiding from pain?'

As far as unfortunate coincidences go, Olive Oil's timing to express warnings was impeccable! In our morning lesson, she informed me of opportunity to have my confession heard by a visiting priest, or as O.O pointed out, a stranger we knew nothing about! In accordance with 'modern thinking', we had the choice of confessing our sins face-to-face or keep to the tradition of relating through a screen. O.O advocated the latter for safety's sake, sharing stories she had heard of some priest's undue advances. As she spoke, I wore a calm, outward appearance, nodding my head at her advice, while inwardly my heart was imitating a ball in a pin-ball machine, flying up to my throat, crashing down into my lungs, even descending all the way to my toes, before bouncing back to its own position. O.O had no idea she was feeding already monstrously excessive fears! Behind the facade of absolute calm, my screwed-up emotions screamed, *'Someone make her shut up!!!'*

In my experience, I had known only 'good priests'; one or two were a little distant, but none ever tried to harm me. Attempting to deal with my fear of man, while the voice of my 'Mistress' told me to fear them was driving me further and further into desperation. When I was first fell in love with Jesus, the priest whom God used to bring me into His presence and disciple me was Fr. May. I'm sure, like the rest of us, he wasn't perfect, but he had the look of an angel at the Charismatic meetings. His eyes, as small as any other human's eyes, seemed to contain vast riches of beauty – the eyes are the gateway to the soul, and what I saw in this man was one who was sold-out for the love of Jesus. I never tired of giving him my attention when he spoke. In my spiritual life, I could still walk in the fruits of that season but I could not remind myself of the goodness of that man. I was too far gone, trapped by ungodly fear!

I also couldn't remember the kind priest, Fr. Michael, who, along with Momma and nephew, Peter, dropped me off to begin my voluntary year with the Sisters. What about Fr. McKieran – hadn't I sent him a Father's Day card in my year as a volunteer? Obviously, he was someone I trusted enough to honour. Surely I could remember! But I couldn't! These 'good priests' were a distant memory; my life was here – Brighton Hall. Distance from the rest of the human race was not measured in miles; I dwelt in some kind of capsule, cocooned by a multitude of elderly sisters who loved me, a world in which very few men entered – and now I'm told the few that do may not be trustworthy!

I went for confession held in the drawing-room beside the chapel. My body straight, my stride purposeful, sending out the customary message of confidence, yet my eyes fearfully scanning the room – find the perpetrator's screen, and sit behind it, watching always for signs of movement; is he about to pounce, how many seconds will it take to get to the door? If he catches me before I get there, will I be able to raise the alarm or will I suffer – a silent lamb to the slaughter! My confession was as quick as possible, besides my heart's confession was my bad attitude to Olive Oil and although she insisted priests were not to be trusted she would always sit with them at meals, talking off their ear, taking a stab at being funny. Perhaps she would be friends with this man behind the screen and he would repeat my confession to her – I could trust no one!

Leaving the drawing-room, needing to release emotional pressure, I went to the kitchen to *'have a laugh'* with Penny, but she was 'in consultation' with Sister Celia. Armed with a calendar and pen, Celia was in organising mode and I would have to wait until dates, times and numbers of guests were finalised before I could have my *'laugh'*. I took a glass of water and leaned on the high, large chrome table, resting my face on the palms of my hands. Maggie-May passed by with dishes from the infirmary. I thought she'd laugh if I tried to trip her up, so stretched out my back leg. Not seeing the obstacle in her way, instead of the slight stumble I was expecting, she fell to the ground, plates crashing about her. Moments passed as the only sound that could be heard was from tin plates mocking as they crashed to the ground to the beat of two, *'You fool! You fool! You fool!'*

Sister Celia was not long in seconding this opinion! After rushing to help up her assistant, she turned to me, 'What on earth did you do that for?'

Maggie-May, dazed, veil skew-whiff, legs wobbling like jelly, insisted, 'It's okay! It's okay! I'm grand! I'm grand!'

I stood there speechless, with a defiant look upon my face; I wanted to say *'sorry'*, but just couldn't find my voice. My face began to glow as brightly as a hot fire. Penny, seeing my embarrassment, removed me from the situation, telling me to pick up the dishes and go wash them in the scullery. After the evening meal, still embarrassed, I was back in the big sink washing a lot more dishes when Maggie-May put her hands on my shoulders, 'Don't worry about this afternoon – it's the kind of silly prank I'd pull. I know you didn't mean any harm by it.'

My face turning beetroot, I formed a small smile, still beating myself up on the inside for my foolish mistake. I only hoped Celia in her fury had not already reported me to O.O. During the next twenty-four hours, my journal began to read as a catalogue of confessions, my skills in community living plummeting to an all-time low, each error magnified in my heart and mind by the fearful possibility of O.O being informed.

It all began with a phone call. Sitting comfortably in the Community phone-box, big enough to present itself as Dr. Who's flying machine, I was chat – chat – chat with Yvonne while Penny was rant – rant – rant, marching up and down the corridor leading to the kitchen. After 30 minutes, my time-travel capsule returned to earth with a bang! Opening the door, Penny's complaint from all the way up the corridor rang out in my ears as clear as a church bell – 'It's not fair, and I'll tell her when she comes back! We've only one phone for all de Sisters in de house and she's hogging it!'

I could not claim ignorance of the rule that phone calls were to be limited to ten minutes, as Penny was present when I promised Sister Celia six weeks earlier I would keep within the limit! I should have been brave enough to face the music! I should have been humble enough to apologise! I should have been selfless enough to inform them the phone was now 'free' for someone else to use! Instead I fled – out the back door and over to my bedroom in the Novitiate. *'They're not like You, Lord. It's hard to forgive seventy-times-seven!'*

I worried before bedtime, anticipating Penny's response, turning my fears into nightmares as I slept, returning to the main-house in the morning full of trepidation. How angry would Penny be? Although Penny was always protective toward me, fear suggested she might be so angry, she'd not only scold me but even report me to O.O.[1] Anxiety burned a hole in my stomach as I avoided Penny, running up the stairs to my work in the infirmary. Yet, when I was sent to the kitchen for the infirm Sisters' mid-morning snack, she was as nice as pie (even her gorgeous apple pie) and never made the slightest suggestion towards her upset from the night before.

Time for elevenses! Along bounds 'Attie (Sister Harriet) with Sister Finnian in tow. Together they lead me to a shelf. Only the day before, on seeing Sister Harriet throwing scraps of material out, I asked her not to throw them away as I could use them. My eyes popped out of my head as I anxiously looked at three hefty bags of scraps sitting on a shelf labelled, 'Do Not Touch – Novitiate'.

'You'll get me killed writing that; you haven't got Sister's permission.'

'I'll see her', she replied.

---

[1] 'I would never have gotten Kaitlyn into trouble! Besides, she was quite capable of doing that all by herself ☺' – Sister Penny.

'Don't you dare', I screamed, thinking, *'My God, I'd be shot at dawn!'*

Sister Finnian, much more sensitive to my situation than 'Attie was, said she was led to believe I knew all about it, and as I didn't want it, 'Attie was to take the sign down. 'Attie, rather put out, ripped off the sign and made a u-turn, chuntering as she disappeared along the corridor, 'Well, you try to help people, and this is the thanks you get!'

Entering the dining room, Sister Aiden was chatting about watching the Opening of Parliament. I was hardly aware of the conversation, deliberating over the trouble 'Attie could get me into. Sister Finnian read this as disinterest, and said so. Although I was actually interested in seeing the Opening of Parliament, as I'd never watched before, I agreed with her assessment. Sister Aiden correcting me, saying I should take interest in that which effects my future, got a blunt reply from me about the wasteful paraphernalia of the upper classes. What should they discuss next, but Mark Thatcher's engagement! I sounded like a real Socialist as I complained about all the media cover for someone simply because he was born to a certain parent! Sister Aiden, the person I most respected in the convent, looked terribly upset with my 'sounding off'. Sister Daniel sitting next to me seemed to understand my need to blow off steam, even if she didn't know the reason behind it, squeezing my hand lovingly as the group sat in silence for a few minutes, afraid to open up another discussion Sister Mary Kaitlyn might blow her top at!

After supper each evening, I was to help clear the dishes in the Novitiate and then go over to the Main House to help put Sister Lucy to bed. That evening, the Sisters were already in the lift and ascending two floors as I came in the front door. I raced up the stairs that encircled the caged lift, meeting the Sisters at the top as Sister Greta pushed open the bendy, criss-cross metal door. Greta was an extremely strong character; having suffered a stroke some years before leaving her left side paralysed, her arm was inoperable, her speech slurred from half the muscles in her face not working, and by sheer determination, she dragged her calliper-cased left leg around with her. She was usually fun to be around, but as a retired nurse, was taking responsibility for the infirmary for a few days while Filis was away with Celia, and our lovely Sister Greta had changed into a demanding monster! Opening the doors, she screamed at me for being late. I being the kind, gentle novice the Sisters had all grown to love and appreciate . . . screamed straight back at her! 'I can't get here any earlier. Besides, Celia will be back soon, and then you'll come out at the normal time!'

I linked Sister Lucy's arm with mine, and without another word, headed toward Lucy's bedroom. The next morning, the old friendly Greta was back. She apologised for her outburst, which enabled me to admit my own fault, and we had fun all morning, laughing at our 'out of character' behaviour. I fought the argument I should be humble enough to apologise to both Sisters Harriet and Aiden, making the excuse an apology to Sister Aiden would sound so trite, and would be for the wrong reason – to gain her respect rather than make her feel any better. I did, however, approach 'Attie to ask her forgiveness. Finding her rummaging through a drawer full of bedclothes, I bumbled around, trying to find the words to express my *first* undirected apology in my whole life.

'Yes dear, what is it?' she asked. 'Do you want some bed sheets?'

When I eventually found the words to apologise, she outdid me in charity.

'No dear, I realised afterwards you were quite right; some-one could have passed a comment.'

I was safe with 'Attie, but someone was definitely telling my every public move to the Novice-Mistress. What puzzled me more than the informant's identity was when and how they did it. Olive Oil left the main-house immediately after mass and meals, and I only once saw her accosted in the corridor on her way out. Most of the Sisters loved me, but still I was very cautious of 'public' relationships. Working in the Infirmary, I became good friends with Filis, newly appointed 'Matron' to Brighton and at twenty-six years old, the youngest professed Sister by far. I missed the fact we never had any privacy, and whoever was reporting me from my work department, must have training in shorthand, not missing one syllable, whether I was in dialogue or ranting a monologue! One of the corrections O.O demanded in my behaviour in the main-house was to stop referring to the nuns by their names without their title Sister. On the first morning I resolved to call everyone Sister, the first four at least were called only by their names. Obviously, my habit was more ingrained than I realised! It became a novelty trying to remember to call them 'Sister', but I wasn't even willing to attempt calling Penny or Filis, Sister; I was too proud, imagining them laughing or making a joke about my becoming *'a good little novice'*.

I began to feel guilty about everything, even my little escapades on the bike evoked private confession to Jesus. I had thought Sister Henrietta who had moved from Brighton to a small village convent nearby seemed a little 'blue', and so decided I would surprise her with a visit.

I did partly go for her sake, she seemed to be feeling lonely, and a bit of attention does us all a world of good, but I also went in the hope of something nice to eat – maybe they'd be having chocolate cake for tea! I'd love my intentions for

*doing good to be pure, but as you can see, they're not! I did
better than I expected – a Mars and a Double Decker!*

*I also went because of the 'danger' element. O.O doesn't
like me roaming the countryside in my green tracksuit, let
alone visit a convent! I wasn't expecting to see all the Sisters
– their absence was going to be my defence if ever
questioned. Now I've got to hope none of them ever tells! The
only person I told was Sister Lucy while I got her ready for
bed, and as she won't remember, she can't split☺. If I tell
anyone else, Olive Oil might find out and bring it into
conversation – lightly as she does, gain my confidence, then
bang, the lion has taken the bait and down goes the cage
door! Looking at the positive, you only cage wild animals
you want to keep; you shoot game outright! (But seriously,
Lord, I think I should have some freedom!)*

As lone-novice, I did have more time outside of Brighton
than novices before me, attending Seminary College twice a
week. Other than all the young men training to be priests,
a young recently professed Sister, Susan, was also attending
the College. We quickly paired up, sitting together in class and
dining room. After lunch one day, Susan and I went for a walk
in the grounds. Before afternoon lessons, we must all attend
Mass in the College chapel, much longer than its width, with
ornate choir pews facing one another, left and right of the
altar. As we entered, neither of my two bodyguards saw us,
presuming we arrived late. Sister Alison accepted the truth
when she questioned me directly. Meanwhile O.O, not hearing
me, using her indirect approach, reminded Susan, amidst
titters, of the time of Mass. Susan assured her we were not
late, but five minutes early. I wondered if my Novice-Mistress
wanted me to sit with her, but I wanted my freedom. All
afternoon I grappled with the concern; do I stay quiet, leaving

her to tell me, or do I *put her first*, and ask her opinion, willing to follow whatever she suggests? As we waited for Sister Alison to collect the car, I found the courage to ask. 'No', she replied, she didn't mind, but I should be careful about walking the grounds after lunch.

'Why? What has happened?' I asked, imagining an axe-murderer loose in the area.

'Nothing', she replied. 'You should just be careful how you use your time. Mother Anastasia arranged for you to come here to study. After lunch, therefore, you should go to the library.'

I will never get used to her application of language! I did, however, dutifully follow her command, going to the library on my next break, not to study but to finish my brother-in-law, Dennis's birthday card (and thought to myself, good job she never knew Susan and I visited the guys' dorm after lunch on our first day☺ She would have surely had a fit!).

9. His Grace Is Sufficient!

At the end of October, Brighton Hall became a hive of activity as it held its Annual Autumn Fair, the best part of this being Sisters visiting from all the other convents. Reuniting with the Sisters from Liverpool was great; especially Sister St. Huggie who, having a soft spot for me, was very protective. I always enjoyed being with my original 'family', the Rescue Sisters. This year, one Sister was added; Rose-Anna had returned from Rome to become 'House Mother' in one of the larger Family Homes (taking 16 children, aged 0–18). In my meeting with Mother Anastasia, she had promised to arrange a visit from Sister Rose-Anna. Most of the Tyrolese Sisters were very pretty, and Rose-Anna was no exception; seeing her for the first time since my visit to Roma, I was so thrilled to spot her in the crowd, radiating beauty! I wanted to give her a big kiss on the cheek, but what would everyone think of me, so I gave only the customary hug. And chatting with Fr. McKieran and his assistant, Fr. Watson was more amusing than watching the *Morecombe and Wise* show!

Before they all arrived, it was a little boring, with nothing to do but look at the prepared stalls. I purchased a hard-backed Jerusalem Bible for only a few pounds; until then I only read the Good News Bible. I was glad to add a more mature edition to my library! With Bible in hand, I made an excuse of taking it over to the Novitiate before I lost it. In truth, I had decided to change my clothes. I may only have the option to wear 'blue' or 'blue', but I had styles for every occasion – work, study, chilling, special and very special (with shoes to match). I wanted to put on one of my 'special' outfits, even though I was technically 'working'. When I returned, I was surprised to meet a pleasant scout called Grant seconded to help me run a stall – I thought it was compulsory for teenagers to be '*off-hand*', yet Grant, such a lovely lad, proved that myth wrong☺.

Sister Krista, having travelled with the Sisters from Chester, remained for a few days. As we chatted over supper in the main-house, I shared a problem confronting me since winter began to descend on Brighton – I kept sleeping-in! I had not realised the depth of my anxiety until I spoke it out; I slept in most mornings and on two occasions in the last week I experienced the embarrassment of Olive Oil waking me. Krista said I should not worry about it, but only that morning Olive Oil had warned me if my bad habit was to continue she would soon be saying something. I had accepted her correction and vowed to sleep early, but as the day moved on and I became tired, I began to fret; to whom would she say something, to me or to Mother Anastasia? With mixed feelings, I wrote to Jesus:

> *If ever I was told to leave, it would be great – my decision*
> *would be made for me! Yet, I felt such great support*
> *today. Everyone is very mindful I am alone, and although*
> *I'm not conscious of their support on a daily basis, I*
> *must have faith; there are a lot of prayers spoken on*
> *my behalf!*

That very night, the clocks were turned back giving me one hour's extra sleep, plus I went to bed 'on time', yet I still slept in! I heard both alarms that I set, but refusing to wake, I continued my time in the land of nod, putting the ringing sound into a dream. I was in a shop, trying out a bell for the door, *'That's right; it should be nice and loud.'*

As the second bell rang, I objected it was too weak to be useful, and on I slept! I was only three minutes late, but I may as well have been three hours late for the trouble this caused. When Olive Oil initially sounded concerned, asking me if I had stayed up late working, I fell into her trap, saying I did other things last thing. She immediately turned on me, correcting me for being so irresponsible. Knowing I had risen often to watch the sunrise in the summer annoyed O.O even more – 'Anyone can get up when the sun is shining. It takes determination to get up in the dark.'

The onset of dark, wintery days as well as nights caused me to long for hibernation. I usually enjoy the cascade of colours in the autumn leaves, but as I walked in the woods, trying to praise God for the beauty of His creation, every falling autumn leaf caused me to weep; I could not take this stripping alone! With darkness descending and an empty 'community room' to welcome me back from my walk, depression drew me to my bed (with the alarm set of course!) My journal, 'Letters to Jesus' became increasingly important, leading me (slowly) in the direction of self-acceptance:

My relationship with O.O is nonexistent! I feel so 'crumby'.
I'm not too interested in forcing conversation! A young
person, or even a funny person, could pull me out of all this
drudgery. It's almost suppertime – I shall have to pull myself
up. Besides, my attitude is not fair on Sister Stevie. I don't

want to handle another lecture from my Novice-Mistress –
to be avoided at all costs!

Although I had many jobs I wanted to do, I was too depressed to attend to any of them that day. On the following two days however, I turned to spring-cleaning to catapult me out of wintery despair. On the third day, when a teenage girl came to visit, exploring the possibility of entering the convent, I had the pleasure of entertaining her – *the usual can-can!* – But seriously, as I spoke with her I realised I was genuinely 'happy'. *'No need to sell her any yarns; my optimism is due to the fact this is where I belong.'*

As if that development wasn't enough, within four weeks of attempting to take Mother Anastasia's advice in praying for my relationship with Olive Oil, the impossible happened. Beginning to refer to her by her real name (on good days☺), I was amazed to record:

> *Trust has evolved and I thank You, Jesus. I enjoyed Sister*
> *Peter's company without reservation for the first time*
> *today. I feel no man-made barrier between us. I feel at ease*
> *with her. I can say, 'Isn't she lovely' to myself while she's*
> *speaking. Her humour is very simple; she loves life. I can*
> *laugh at her jokes; I can laugh with her. I even think I*
> *can sympathise with her. It is nothing less than a miracle.*
> *Thank You, Jesus!*

On 1st November, I was more excited to celebrate my first year's anniversary of moving to Brighton than the day in which I celebrated my entrance into the Convent. No one understood my joy; they all thought I was relieved a year was over, but I was jubilant that my fears of the Novitiate were greater than the reality;

The heavy, heavy load has gone. I am as free as a bird and as light as a feather. You love me, Lord, and I belong here. And I am happy in my belonging. Praise You Lord!

This is the year of spiritual formation with many years to follow. I don't want to waste my time worrying when I should be trusting, cribbing when I should be praising, bitching when I should be loving! Will You help me become the person You want me to be?

Over the coming months, I would bounce back and forth between happiness in believing I was called to be a nun and despair in failing the practicalities of Novitiate living. One morning, Olive Oil woke me after morning prayers were over. As I descended the stairs, I was petrified as I saw her standing at the door looking out for Sister Alice collecting us for college. *'Lord, please protect our relationship!'* On seeing me approach, Olive Oil called me to look at the Morning Star. I was so grateful for her compassion, but days later, she told me how she was fuming, and looked at the Morning Star to calm herself. I internally corrected myself; my behaviour must change!

Wet Sundays became a menace to me, presenting me with the longest afternoons in my life! When Yvonne was with me, we often did our own thing in our free afternoons, but at some time we'd meet for a bit of banter. Now alone, I descended the Novitiate stairs, collected food from the kitchen for my ritual Sunday afternoon binge, and entered the deserted 'community' room to study the book of Isaiah.

Isaiah is a book in the Old Testament that, throughout my life, Jesus speaks through, almost as much as He relates to me through the gospels of His own life story as a Man. Like a miniature Bible, Isaiah has 66 chapters splitting into 39 chapters (like the Old Testament) warning a rebellious people of God's wrath, and 27 chapters (like the New Testament) telling of God's love in providing forgiveness through the sacrifice of the life of His Son, Jesus. It always amazed me that God would share with 'a mere man' His plan to send Jesus into the world *in seven hundred years time!* Talk about foreknowledge! Yet, it's within the earlier section, in chapter 6, amidst all the judgement, that I found one of my favourite stories in the Bible. In God's presence, Isaiah recognised he had unclean lips, and in response to his cry, an angel was sent with 'holy coal' to cleanse him. I too wanted the holy coal to touch my lips, cleansing me from defilement. My tongue in 'community' very rarely revealed this deep desire, but in the inner chamber of my heart, I longed to be pure! Furthermore, from the first time I heard God's call, *'Whom shall we send'*, with childlike simplicity and with the burning enthusiasm of Isaiah, I raised my hand quickly into the air – *'O, Lord, send me!'*

As I opened God's Word, I wondered had God said all He wanted to say through the characters of the Bible or were their words written as benchmarks indicating the level to which we are all invited. My thoughts were interrupted by the swinging of the gate and two friendly faces peering into the community room, giving a wave as they headed to the front door. Our room was set to host community, for the afternoon at least! The smallness of the space, perhaps, led the carload from Chester, to enter the ark in shifts – two by two! I totally enjoyed the break from loneliness, and the excitement of having visitors, yet no one could help noticing my quietness. Even I could not distinguish whether I was simply caught in 'reflective mode' or Sister Peter's presence held me in check, she needing to squeeze every word out of me – 'What was that story, Sister Mary Kaitlyn?'

I much preferred listening to our visitors' stories, but listening to one young postulant say that if anyone was going anywhere, she would instantly join them, stirred up pangs of jealousy in me,

> *I wouldn't take their freedom from them. I'd just like a little adventure, that's all! I know my place is here. As Carlo Carretto says, 'The greatest adventure is the search for God.' I belong here; I accept it, but inside I'm a little churned. I'd like to be gallivanting – I'd like You to teach me to 'gallivant' within. Search my soul, Lord.*

I'd like to tell you about the great adventures this led to in the Spirit, but my focus was still on adventure in the natural world. Waking the day before Bonfire Night, I strongly desired to connect with the comfort of childhood – the glowing fire, warm potatoes, tasty toffee apples and the beautiful display of shapes and colours in the fireworks. Even the Catherine Wheel, which my brother annually informed me, represented the story of Catherine, my namesake, being martyred, appeared beautiful to me as vibrant colours and majestic patterns shot off in all directions from the shed door with purpose and determination. Paddy would give detail of Catherine's execution in as much gore as he could express, and he and his friends would burst out laughing as I would squirm at his description – 'They stretched her out, nailing her hands and feet to that wheel, then spun her like a roulette wheel before . . . '

Lifting his two hands up around his face for added effect and popping his eyes out towards me, he would torment, 'They'd burn her alive.'

At this point, Mum would normally be informed and Paddy would get a clip round the ear. 'Stop the scary stories; just light the wheel!'

Lighting the wheel with the long flex, Paddy would shout, 'There she goes, our Kaitlyn, if she doesn't stop being so holy! Isn't that right, boys?'

Paddy, forever the performer, would be quick to prise the wheel from the shed's hold and throw it to land at my feet. 'I'm only telling you for your own good; you need to stop being so holy. You don't want to end up like her, do you?'

I was only small and quite afraid, but I was impressed by Catherine's story; why be a little light shining in the darkness if you can be a brightly coloured spinning flame, twirling 360° through the world! And why not stand up for what you believe in! Now I would stand up for my rights in the Novitiate, even if it was only expressed in attending a bonfire (you know what they say: don't despise small beginnings!). I asked Filis if she would like to accompany me. She said she would, so I asked Josepi to ask Mrs. Pudding if she knew of a local public bonfire, and asked Penny to ask Tony the postman the same question. Meeting Tony the milkman by the backdoor, I asked him directly.

My mother used to tell me as a child, 'When you're all grown-up, you'll be able to go to de moon for your holidays.'

During that morning, I remarked to myself I could be the organiser of those holidays! Only one problem – I wouldn't be allowed to go! In all my enthusiasm, I had forgotten one important detail – I was a novice, and novices, like children, do not make decisions! It seems Penny and Filis forgot too, not pointing out the obvious to me! Yet, sitting with Filis at the end of my duties for the morning, when my Novice-Mistress appeared, I considered how unusual it was for her to be across at the main-house at this time, even more unusual for her to be up in the Infirmary. God must have sent her to seal my plans☺. Asking permission had never gotten me anywhere; the casual, but confident approach would perhaps work better!

'Oh, Sister, Sister Filis and I are just arranging to go to a local bonfire tonight – if that's ok.'

O.O's pale face began to show life, little pink spots forming amidst the determined frowns as she deliberately popped out her eyes to express shock. *Oh! Oh!* 'It's almost time for your lesson. Begin walking over to the Novitiate and I'll catch up with you. I just want a word with Sister Filis.'

'But . . . '

'Now!' she politely but firmly commanded.

I glanced nervously back at Filis, but could not make eye contact as she looked into her half-filled cup of tea. Once out of the building I ran up to the Novitiate, I wasn't going to face the embarrassment of O.O catching up with me!

Ten minutes later, when we met in the living room, she obviously tried hard to remain calm while correcting me – 'Your words were not courteous. I would like you to remember how to make a request. You ask, "May I."'

Considering a request beginning with 'May I' to be both middle-class and subservient, I inwardly vowed, *'I will never say "May I"!'* Outwardly, I nodded.

The pink little fury spots on her face, flashing on and off like twinkling Christmas tree lights, began to fade as she added, 'Sister Filis should have been the one to ask my permission.'

I sat silently, but inside I shouted, *'No way!'* I bowed my head like a corrected schoolchild, a part of me wanting to be able to submit to her authority without all this inward turmoil.

Appearing to mellow, Sister Peter added, 'I will think about it and give you my answer this afternoon. Now, let us begin our lesson.'

I sat embarrassed, wondering how Filis was, but somehow had to put the episode out of my mind to do the work asked of me. At supper, Sister Peter told me she had given it much thought, but as she could see no gain in my going to the bonfire, her answer remained 'no', I could not go. She went on to tell a story now familiar to me of how whenever she or her sister messed-up, they would turn to the other and declare 'I'm a failure', then together they would laugh while reciting their chorus, 'but a happy failure!' When I first heard that story, I thought *What a pathetic pair!* But by now I had warmed to Sister Peter's character and was grateful that she used her skill of implication to suggest that while I had failed to do things correctly, I should still be happy.

> *Lord, I accept her decision. Asking the way I did made me realise I am not so much afraid of Sister Peter as of losing my independence and becoming obedient, but I've given my life to God, and no one has authority over me unless the Father gives it. I must give in; my stubbornness must be put to flight!*

Within three days, I was willing to accept the foolishness of my mistake in trying to take control, but more importantly, in being willing to learn by my mistakes, I could see I was able to enter into the supernatural gift of Jesus' joy, albeit fluctuating, experiencing His joy in waves.

> *Joy is a supernatural gift and so, in my humanity, I cannot understand it, but it's there for the taking, so yes Lord, I wish to receive it. This morning I couldn't help but worry; the Novitiate is a nerve-wracking place! Olive Oil teaches with her eyes and facial expressions. The worst part of this training is the turmoil within – one can't help but wonder if one is doing things right! This wondering, for me, leads to anxiety. Yet, you stayed with me. The answer to every problem is in the Bible, especially the Gospels. Therefore,*

no one has authority over me without the Father first giving
it. I am free. The Father takes all my worries. I am free to be
happy. Grant me a joyful heart, Lord, so that I may give my
life generously to You!

Continuing my journey through the Gospels the next day,
I read the Beatitudes, remarking herein lay a lifetime of
teaching. When I asked Jesus who He was referring to when
He said 'those who mourn', I believe He replied, *'Those who*
mourn for the world, taking the sins and sadness of the world into
their own hearts and asking My forgiveness on their behalf.' I understood that if we will mourn in this way, as Jeremiah did,
embracing the responsibility of a guilty nation even though
he was not personally guilty, the people for whom we mourn
will be comforted with God's love and forgiveness. As I tried
to understand every Bible reading in the context of my life in
the Novitiate, my resolve to relate 'correctly' towards my
Novice-Mistress remained erratic. Meditating on St. Paul's
teaching on love after hearing it in the Office of Readings, I
commented to Jesus,

> *It's beautiful; truly Your words, but how difficult to put into*
> *practice! Love is patient and kind. Love bears all things,*
> *believes all things, hopes all things, endures all things, Love*
> *never fails (how's that possible?) I have come to believe you*
> *don't have to like someone to love her – liking is an emotion,*
> *love is an action; it is charity. I can love Sister Peter. I'll*
> *never like everything about her. I don't like everything about*
> *my family, but I love them!*

As I went to chapel, I resolved to behave with discretion,
repeating to myself, I don't need to like her; I just need to
accept her! Seeing Olive Oil at the chapel door, and Sister

Alison heading to the seat before her, I immediately complained to myself, *'Huh! I have to sit next to her!'*

Looks like I still have some work to do on my new resolution!

When 20th November arrived, Sister Peter made the greatest of fuss, preparing a special breakfast, giving me gifts and showering me with praise for having reached the six-month anniversary of being a novice. I appreciated all her encouragement, but privately found the calculations depressing; six months gone, twelve months left! It wasn't that I thought the period ahead of me too long; on the contrary, I feared it would go too quickly without me learning what God planned to teach me. Looking back at my six months, I could see I had wasted a lot of time in stubbornness, including not allowing the Novice-Mistress to see me in private prayer. On this anniversary, I could see that to some degree I had overcome my stubbornness, now able to sit in the Novitiate chapel for well over an hour, even with Sister Peter right beside me!

I'm tempted to call it a miracle, but whether it is or not, it is certainly Your grace! I'm hoping I'll be graced with many gifts that I may become graceful in the giving.

10. Be Kind to One Another

As November bade us adieu, I was settled in College, enjoying the challenge of lectures and the freedom Sister Peter gave me in the dining room and common room between lessons to establish new friendships; I liked the feeling of 'making it on my own'. I was settled in Brighton too, enjoying the challenge of completing many jobs in the infirmary, and enjoying the company of both infirm and able bodied elderly Sisters.

It will be nice if I'm ready to move on next year, but for now, I'm happy to be here. I love the Sisters spoiling me. It means so much to Daniel to give me her fruit in secret – she feels important. Our faces beam with smiles, her eyes sparkle as we exchange her gift for my gratitude. A small detail, but important to us. We can only love where we're at, and I don't want to be anywhere else.

When I received a padded envelope from a lovely lady, Dinah, whom I had met on my return journey from Rome, I was quick to declare the gifts within, an unusual and expensive silver cross plus £10. Before I should be instructed to give the cross away, I quickly suggested it become a present for Momma. This was agreed and Sister Peter took the £10 for Novitiate funds. I was satisfied with the outcome, enjoying my taste of freedom in poverty, and glad I was moving toward obedience.

Sister Peter broke my thoughts – 'Is there anything you need that you could buy with this money?'

I blushed before answering, 'I could do with some underwear.'

On having the money returned to me, I excitedly shared with Jesus,

I have a whole £10 and permission to spend it in town – would have preferred Stratford-upon-Avon, but Evashall will do!☺

A letter from my Momma, however, created a much sadder reaction within me. Each of my siblings, set up with their own family, had not, as yet, invited Mum for Christmas, and Mum, not wanting to foist herself on them, planned to stay home with a newly acquired kitten. I was heartbroken at the thought of Momma sharing Christmas with a little cat! I imagined her crying as she wrote,

If you were at home, there'd only be you and me. Think how lucky you are. You have the real message of Christmas where you are.

I knew Momma didn't really want to be alone and I didn't want her to be alone either. I considered the only possible option, the one place she wouldn't be intruding, would be with me – and my big welcoming family☺. I began to pray – for courage to ask the Novice-Mistress permission to invite

Momma for Christmas. She might say 'no', but at least I would know. If I didn't ask, I'd no doubt be told later, Momma could have come if I had mentioned her situation!

After twenty-four hours of pleading before the Lord, sometimes with tears, just before descending the stairs for my lesson with Sister Peter, I managed to hand over the whole situation to Jesus, immediately being filled with joy. In an instant, I believed Mum would have a lovely Christmas, wherever she spent it; I knew that I knew Jesus answered my prayer! On entering the community room the first thing out of my Novice-Mistress's mouth was, 'What about your Mum coming down after Christmas?'

I immediately revealed Mum's situation. In response, Sister Peter didn't feel she had the authority to invite Mum for Christmas, but looking forward to visiting would, she suggested, lift Mum's spirits and carry her through Christmas. The offer was more than I had hoped for, so I quickly wrote home with the good news.

At the same time, I was so glad to attend the Charismatic prayer meeting set up by some of the Sisters, becoming oblivious to those around me as I received a fresh infilling of God's peace, joy and love. My heart was so full of praise for Him! I had found life in Jesus through the Charismatic renewal and from the moment of my new birth, there was no looking back! The third Friday night in November 1981 is etched on my soul for all eternity. My friend, Krys, told me she was accompanying a mutual school-friend, Caroline, to a prayer meeting where Caroline expected to be healed from a broken leg. I immediately enthused, 'Oh, I'll come.'

'No', Krys objected, knowing my utter dislike of being touched. 'You wouldn't like it – they touch and hug one another.'

'Don't worry about me', I insisted, 'I will keep them at arm's length!'

I expected a handful of people at the gathering, but instead there were near to three hundred people – for a prayer meeting! Not only that, but also the whole section on the right was full of youths. We were led to the front row, and from there, Krys and I sat on the pew looking at these young people waving their arms around and singing in a funny language between songs. Krys and I laughed and laughed, alternating our vision between the weird behaviour before us and one another. I so respect those youths, for our reaction did not change their behaviour, nor did they seem offended; in the midst of their worship, they just smiled at us, accepting our behaviour. All of a sudden, as we again glanced at one another, Krys and I simultaneously began to cry. These were not tears of correction; in that moment I knew God loved me. In the tea-break before the 'healing session', Caroline asked for prayer, as we needed to catch buses to go home. Sitting with her leg up on a bench, a group of about twelve youths joined Fr. May, the leader, to pray with her. When the prayers were finished Caroline excitedly ran with cast-encased leg, full pelt, around the building shouting, 'I'm healed! I'm healed!'

Fr. May turned his attention to Krys and me, asking if we would like prayer. Krys, looking bewildered by the whole event, declined, but I agreed. I was asked to kneel, and with the youths surrounding me, praying in their funny language, Fr. May began to ask for Jesus and the Holy Spirit to come. My body began to feel pressure to 'fall'. I had never seen anyone 'slain in the Spirit' so didn't know this was a 'normal' response to prayer in Charismatic circles. With all the strength I could muster, I held myself up until I could fight no more. The minute I touched the ground, my life was completely transformed! I'd always believed in Jesus and grew up in awe of Almighty God, but in one moment my spirit was renewed, my soul cleansed as I personally encountered Jesus' love; He'd come to live in my heart and my life would never be the same again! Even Holy Spirit had arrived on the scene, saturating – immersing – baptizing me in Himself. 'Funny words' now cascaded out of my mouth – Holy Spirit had given me His gift of a Heavenly language, also known as 'tongues'.[1] On that third Friday night in November 1981 at about 8.45p.m., I was invited to begin life all over again; the cork was removed and joy was bubbling right out of me!☺

By the time I was ready to arise from my private time with Jesus, only one person was by my side, praying for me – Tiny Tina. I stood up and hugged her, thanking her for her prayers. As I walked down the street, Caroline running ahead and circling back in excitement at her healing, I continuously hugged Krys, the only topic on my lips, that which had captured my heart; the overwhelming love of God. Krys, truly puzzled, could only say, 'I don't understand; you don't like to be touched!'

When I arrived home, the girl who refused Momma the pleasure of gratitude for gifts in the form of a hug for many a year, bound into the living room, smothering her in hugs and kisses.

'You've been on drugs!' Mum accused.

'No, Mum, I've been to church.'

'No one comes home from church like that!'

I did! And I went again and again and again to keep on getting this incredible touch from God. I thought the training I received 'normal'; I didn't know anything else, but later I could see what an incredible blessing I experienced. We met together on a Friday evening for an all-generation meeting.

---

[1] See 1 Corinthians 12:4, 7–11

People came from different areas and denominations in search of answers to prayer. One Dominican monk, committed to a cloister-life of prayer, was dying when the Abbot allowed him to come to a meeting in the hope of a miracle. I remember the stretcher being brought in and taken along the left side of the church (away from us noisy youngsters on the right!☺) I also remember him giving testimony of receiving his healing! Healed, alleluia! My faith was so high after that, nothing was impossible for God! When the television broke, I saw no need for an electrician to fix it. My sister Trisha beside me, we prayed that television back into working order! When a young child, Shane, next door was so sick with fever and the doctor told his mother there was nothing he could do, Marion turned to me for prayer. We went to his cot, prayed for Jesus to heal, and Shane instantaneously jumped to his feet, full of life, and with his arms outstretched, cried, 'Mummy', which when translated means, 'Get me out of here; I've got toys to play with and food to eat!'

In both the Friday evening meeting and the youth meeting on Sunday afternoons, we would take time to sit in God's presence and listen. No talking to God, just listening! Then a microphone would be passed around and people could share a word or picture the Holy Spirit imprinted on their hearts. It was great training; encouraged, I would spend time daily in God's presence, learning to listen to His heartbeat. God introduced the gift of prophecy to me in poetic language. As prior to my new life in Christ, the only time I got a good grade in poetry was the day I cheated, copying a poem from a book, I would never question *'Is this God?'* when poetry formed in my head; it had to be!

As well as these two meetings, young people who wanted to go deeper in their walk with God could join a discipleship class with the Maltfriscans (the abbreviation of Maltby [the town] and Franciscans [the rule the youth group followed]). If you look at St. Paul's letters to the Ephesians and Philippians, you will see both letters split into two – first the spiritual lesson, then the practical. That was what the discipleship classes were like. We would be taught the word, and then our homework would be to put our learning into practice. One time, being challenged to 'evangelise' during the week, I eventually plucked up the courage to approach a man who travelled on the same bus as me every night, asking, 'Do you know Jesus loves you?'

I was shocked to receive his reply, 'Yes'. I hadn't received training for that answer, so simply responded, 'Good', before taking my usual seat a few rows behind him!

I wasn't attending these meetings very long when I felt a burden for the youth in my own parish. As a family, we had recently moved to the area, so I didn't even know all the youths, but I believed strongly Jesus wanted me to lead a youth meeting. Fr. Michael, encouraging this, gave me the names and addresses of youths in the area, and a regular weekly meeting was soon underway. A 'young-at-heart' Charismatic chap in the parish, Vincent Brown, didn't think the older ones should miss out on that which God had placed within me, so asked for a meeting for all generations. I remember climbing the steep hill to the church, absolute trepidation almost rolling me back down again! Halfway up the hill, I stopped and asked Jesus for a word to strengthen me in my journey, instead of 'bolt' as my soul wanted to do,

Do not let anyone look down on you because you are young, but be an example for the believers in your speech, your conduct, your love, faith and purity.

(1 Timothy 4:12 GNB)

I received boldness to continue the steep climb and lead the meeting.

Thanks to Fr. May lending me money to pay the fees, I also attended A Level Scripture Studies. The class consisted of white Evangelicals and black Pentecostalists. The Evangelicals tended to believe the Bible would teach us how to behave without every story being true or agreeing those things should happen today. My beliefs related more to the Pentecostalists, asserting the Word is 100% true in both historical facts and the promises presented to us, sharing a love of and dependency on Holy Spirit to manifest these promises. Our teacher, with a twinkle in his eye, would stir up a debate deliberately 'proving' the inconsistency of Scripture. He trained us well, demanding we speak from knowledge of Scripture, not hearsay or emotion. When I moved to Chester, to live in community with the Volunteers, I led a Charismatic meeting in our chapel each week. It's amazing how God can turn the tables, as my Religious Education teacher from school, Sister Paul (a sweet, lovely Sister of Mercy nun), who happened to be training as a nurse near by, attended the meetings I led.

Three years later, joining my Sisters in their meeting, I prayed for Jesus to send His Spirit upon this small group. After the meeting, I shared with Sister Celia my belief that the Lord wanted them to set up a core-group. In two weeks, having received confirmation, Celia was ready to set it up, asking if anyone wanted to join the core-group that would meet half-an-hour before the general meeting. I had been adamant within that I wasn't going to impose my past experience on them. I knew I was very blessed in my rich foundations of the Charismatic Renewal, but I also knew I had a tendency to 'take control'; it was better for me to concentrate on taking part!

I'll never enjoy my chosen life as a lamb when I keep trying to be a shepherd!

Heading to the woods, feeling guarded by the tall pine trees protectively lining the path, I passed beyond the clear lake toward my favourite spot, the willow tree. Standing close to the trunk, I felt secure, 'under the shadow of the Almighty'. For three days, Jesus had been assuring me I need not be afraid. Looking at the willow's branches representing the 'fingers of God', He assured me I'm safe in His arms. Looking beyond those 'fingers' to the water, He assured me I'm safe, I won't drown.

I have to learn to act according to Your word and at the moment You lovingly, gently say 'do not be afraid'. What comes through very much is Your patience. You repeat Your word again and again waiting for me to respond. I pray for the grace to respond fully, to live the gospel, to trust You, Lord God.

During my visit at least, I was able to let go of fear and be filled with peace. God wanted more for me, chipping away at my inner-discontentment,

My child, stop doing; just learn to 'be'!
You don't have to prove yourself to Me.
Your imperfections don't stop Me from loving you.
Please accept yourself, for you know that I do.

Deciding it was better that I not go to the core-group meeting, I sat in the community room, passing the time before attending the prayer meeting. That, I'm sure, was the right decision, but when Sister Alison heading to the meeting a few minutes late, asked if I was coming, I went along. We entered a silent room. I wanted to know what was happening, but didn't ask. Celia breathed a deep sigh and shared, 'All I can think of is "God's healing power" – I'm too tired to think!'

I waited another minute, and then broke the silence in saying I didn't feel the meeting should be so much planning, but praying; we shouldn't be racking our brains!

Sister Celia took another deep sigh! 'We're not racking our brains. We were praying for enlightenment of the Holy Spirit *before* you came in and that's what I got!'

Dear Lord,

I need to learn discretion! I need to be part of the group before I go attempting to reform it! Because they weren't praying aloud, I didn't think they were praying. It seems to me the only person not praying was me! I felt Your forgiveness immediately; You offered me peace, and the Sisters' forgiveness followed. I ask for this gift of forgiveness for I must learn to forgive myself.

I always seemed to put my foot in it when it came to Sister Celia! Recent renovations in the kitchens and dining room caused havoc in the convent, and to top it all, one of the elderly Sisters had to be buried (because she had died, of course, not for any misdemeanour!). Wanting to encourage Sister Celia at the end of a demanding day, I found her in the kitchen unwinding with Penny and Maggie-May.

'Well done, Sister', I began, 'you've done a great job today, coping with everything!'

If you could have seen the looks on their faces! I suppose it might have been okay if my voice didn't sound like a performance!

Sister Celia, stunned, soon bounced back, deciding to join the act – 'Thank you, dear; you've done a marvellous job too!'

I hadn't done anything! Making a swift U-turn, I exited the kitchen quicker than I entered, aware of how foolish I sounded. Sister Aiden, whom I had tried to emulate as I spoke to Celia, was a respected figure with the right to congratulate people on fulfilling their roles; I was a novice, bottom of the rung! I can't say I felt any less foolish for my words in the core-group, but everyone was gracious toward me, perhaps recognising I meant no harm.

The following day, in preparation for Advent, we had a 'day of recollection' led by Fr. Gilbert from Keele University. I was amazed at how perfectly Fr. Gilbert's talks fit not only with the Mass readings but also scripture Jesus revealed to me in my private prayer time. Together they were the ingredients of a powerful day. Speaking on community living, Fr. Gilbert both encouraged and challenged us to improve ourselves individually for the sake of the whole Body while Jesus personally asked me to put on the whole armour of God (Ephesians 5:10–20). In recognising I do not fight against flesh and blood, but against spiritual powers and control, I must guard my heart, my mind, my spirit, and my walk, wielding the word of God, the sword of the Spirit, with my tongue, rather than the bitter deluge that had escaped my mouth hitherto!

Recognising fear of man is related to fear of shame, rooted in pride, I could see inverted pride caused me, while liking my Novice-Mistress in the privacy of my heart, to continue to defy God's direction and criticise her behind her back, too proud to face anyone ridiculing me for having become 'a proper little novice'. I wondered if confessing to Sister Peter as soon as I committed my sin would break the cycle. Talking this over with Fr. Gilbert, he advised against it; reminding someone of things forgotten, ignored or even unknown could serve no good purpose!

*The worst of it is I do respect her and am enjoying my
Novitiate – I love the Sisters and have time to be with You.
Don't You wish I'd take the opportunity! Instead I gossip.
Everything's fine; what do I find to gossip about? The Past!
Lord, it's behind me; I have to reach to the future! If I can't
keep my own counsel, I'll have to keep away from my
friends, in the evenings at least!*

There was one person with whom I could comfortably share my new **true** feelings about my Novice-Mistress – Sister Caris! The thought of ringing her first came into my mind as I was making Christmas cards in the late afternoon, but as only half of the four months had passed in which I had privately vowed not to contact her, I objected; two months to go yet! As I prepared Sister Lucy for bed, the thought came again, receiving the same adamant refusal. As I later sat in the chapel, trying to read, an argument began to form in my mind; I had set four months as a target, but surely the most important objective was for my contact **not** to be 'needs based'. I was in a good place emotionally and had the amazing news my relationship with the Novice-Mistress was good. Reaching a satisfactory conclusion, I made my way to Dr. Who's space travel machine at the back door of the convent to send my voice to Chester.

'The two of you have such different characters', Sister Caris encouraged, 'it has taken time for you to recognise the good in one other.'

In preparation for the Chapter, a very important meeting taking place every six years in which regional leaders come together to discuss the future of the Order and appoint the top leadership, each community is sent a number of differently coloured papers containing questions to be discussed and answers submitted. At the beginning of December, the first of the papers arrived, the 'green paper' on 'Government'. The three bodies attending our Novitiate meeting were of course the Novice-Mistress, Sister Stevie and me. I was amazed how I had changed, and not for the better! In prayer, I had sought God's answers. I knew I had received them, putting pen to paper to write wisdom beyond my own ability, but sharing those insights? That was a totally different matter! I, who as a schoolgirl, had participated in Public Speaking competitions, was barely able to string together the sentences I had written. With a lack of confidence and even less respect for myself, absolutely overcome with fear of revealing anything of my inner self, I was hardly able to breathe, stuttering my way through the answers.

The next day Sister Peter came to my room with a couple of messages. 'One other thing . . . '

'Oh, Lord!'

'Sister Stevie was . . . '

'Oh, God, what's coming?' Knowing she used Sister Stevie's 'thoughts and opinions' to correct me, I finished the sentence in my head, 'Upset you didn't bring any oranges from the main-house yesterday.'

Amazingly, her sentence didn't go at all like that!

'Sister Stevie was saying how impressed she was at your contribution yesterday – and I was too. You obviously put a lot of thought and consideration into what you said. You have strong convictions. You will be a great help to the congregation if you follow those convictions.'

Rather shocked by this affirmation, I nonetheless knew 'If' was a very large word containing a lot of dynamite – she frightened me, knowing there and then, I had not heard the last on the subject of my convictions!

I hated her referring to my actions, so I felt annoyed even as she affirmed, 'It's lovely to see the change in you.'

I could say nothing but my annoyance increased as she continued, 'Not just being in chapel', she pointed in its direction, 'but seeing the fruits from your prayer-time. So many people have mentioned it; how you have changed. I think it's wonderful to watch God grace people.'

This last sentence immediately calmed my soul; she was neither praising me nor taking the credit for my change, but praising God for His grace. Without it, I would have probably fought spending private prayer time in chapel for some weeks, defiance rising up to battle. In fact, it didn't take much to have defiance raise its ugly head!

That evening when I returned from the main-house, Sister Peter told me how she had 'oiled' the spin-dryer and it no longer squeaked. 'I thought we'll encourage Sister Mary Kaitlyn to do some washing.'

I, as usual, was shocked by her assumption – what the eye can't see the imagination can't register! As we spoke, a bag hung over my shoulder containing a few clothes washed only two days before and freshly ironed while I waited for Sister Lucy during her long visit to the bathroom. I was much more comfortable, 'living' in the main-house where I had a community to which I could belong. When I did my ironing in the evenings, I would see Penny's neat pile of clothing she had ironed in the afternoon before rushing off to present afternoon-tea. I warmed toward Penny's working-class roots, coming from County Tipperary in Ireland as my father did, and wondered how a country-bumpkin could make her years-old laundry look like new clothes sitting on a 'Mark's and Spencer's' shop-shelf!

The sewing machine was in the same quarters, and so again, I would use that one instead of the one in the Novitiate.

Sister Cleo came along one afternoon and presented me with the most beautiful set of sewing needles, an heirloom passed down to her from her mother. The three-fold leather-bound, brown purse, held an extensive range of needles each complete with a shiny brass head. I knew, in my call to poverty, I should not receive such a gift. I also knew if I asked my Novice-Mistress's permission to keep the gift, I would be refused. Yet, 'loving the gift' I decided to stay quiet, and hoped Sister Cleo would do the same, promising her I would cherish her gift always (which, of course, is still in my possession☺).

The one part of the convent I never cared to revisit was the laundry set aside for personal washing; a large dark, musky basement room. As I spin-dried my jumpers, I worried they had the 'plague' as small, solid pieces would descend into the bowl awaiting water. Without enough light to discern if these creatures were living or dead, I would flee, racing up the stairs, leaving emptying the bowl to somebody else! For that reason, I conceded to do my hand washing in the Novitiate. Before my Novice-Mistress spoke, I intended to wash the next day, but she was going on a four-day trip to London in only a few days, I could wait; I would not give her the satisfaction of hearing that spin-dryer humming! After she left, I washed all my clothes with Pirate Radio blaring at the highest volume. The only other difference in my time while she was away was that Sister Alison offered to take me shopping in the city after College. I appreciated her kindness more than I did visiting the shops! When my Novice-Mistress returned on 9th December, I recorded in my letters to Jesus:

Sister Peter came back today. I just could not believe our reunion! It wasn't lively or boisterous, but we both were genuinely pleased to see one another. At the moment, I'm floating inside a big bubble – it's called Your love, and

nothing can distract me from the joy it brings. On the
contrary, people who see this balloon in action, find joy too.
Your love is boundless.

There is a certain degree of tension, though. I watch her
every action and reaction. I expect a scolding in every
situation, but maybe that's just part of being in the
Novitiate. It won't last forever; less than a year left together
and we share more joy than all the negative aspects that
come into our relationship. I no longer need to tell myself I
can like her; I already do. Thank You Lord God for that gift
– it brings an inner peace.☺

Two days later, I enjoyed the responsibility of taking care
of the infirmary while the community discussed the 'green
paper'. I hoped Sister Stevie, as representative of the Novitiate,
would not mention my name when sharing perceptions from
the Novitiate (there were three of us in the meeting), but
apparently she went to great lengths to highlight Sister Mary
Kaitlyn's insights not once or twice, but on every issue
discussed! Landing in the dining room for afternoon-tea (not
that I'm a tea-drinker myself, but I'm always first in line for
the accompanying treat!) – Anyway, as I arrive all the Sisters
begin to tell me how impressed they are with my understanding of Governmental issues.

'By the time you're in your 40s you'll be the Mother
General, no doubt about it!'

'You never know, she might become Mother General in her
30s – our youngest yet!'

Now, on the one hand, I adored praise from all my 'Granny'
nuns, but on the other, I knew at some point, I'd have a hefty
price to pay for such high praise! The following day, leaving
the main-house on our first beautiful snow-clad day of winter,
my boots crunching the ground below, the sun mildly shining

mid-way in the sky, I made my way happily to the Novitiate carrying one pint of milk, half a dozen eggs from Josepi's hens and – the reason for my joy – a gorgeous apple pie from Penny! *'All for me, all for me'* I sang to myself with glee. Olive Oil, even though she was built like a stick was always watching her weight[2] and Sister Stevie didn't eat much pastry, but I could eat for England when it came to Penny's delicious apple pie – sweet, sweet filling inside crispy light pastry.

My joy soon turned to sorrow as in the afternoon lesson the appointed time had obviously been reached for O.O to strike the first blow! 'Convictions are pointless if you won't put them into action! You can hear a sermon, but it's not of any use if you're not listening. It is no good respecting people without following their examples. You know what I'm leading up to . . . '

I didn't have a clue!

Quite simply, my convictions being voiced about in the main-house were 'nothing but hot air'; I had no right to be receiving all this praise when I could not even get out of bed in the mornings. What would the Sisters think of that if they knew and how can my apology ever be taken seriously when the next day I sleep in again! Her correction over, she obviously wanted to finish her analysis on a good note, assuring me that, for all my faults, I had changed – I was more thoughtful.

The problem with that kind of observation always has the opposite effect than the one intended; instead of encouraging me with the assertion of today, I'm disheartened by the impression I made yesterday! However, if I am to be a

[2] **Footnote of Fairness:** 'Sr. Peter' is not remembered as being figure-conscious, but took 'mortification' seriously – whether of food or emotions. Being very controlled, she therefore, found it harder to understand spontaneity in God's service. (Sister Representative)

happier person tomorrow I must accept the person of
yesterday. I am on a spiritual journey, one in which You,
my Lord, are leading me!

Within days, listening to the BBC Radio News while we ate
our supper, a report of an escapee convict from a local prison
came across the airwaves, causing a veil of fear to cover Olive
Oil's face. I casually suggested that offering accommodation
to such a person would be a great opportunity to share the
love of Jesus and bring him to Christ.

My Novice-Mistress turned every shade of green as she
retorted, 'Sister Mary Kaitlyn, do not think we are going to
open our door to a convict! You heard the report – he's
dangerous!'

'Perfect love casts out fear – Jesus would protect us', I replied.

'If we see such a man, we will call the Police – do I make
myself clear?'

Now the chameleon camouflage on her face turned a most
sickly yellow as, with exasperation, Olive Oil's head and
shoulders collapsed into the back of her chair. Sister Stevie
all-of-a-sudden became incredibly sprightly, jumping up from
her seat and dashing off in the direction of the kitchen offering
to pour Sister Peter another cup of tea – with extra sugar!

I picked up my half-eaten sausage roll, mumbling, 'I was
just saying!'

Looking over at my Novice-Mistress breathing deeply while
her eyes searched the ceiling for answers, I was initially
somewhat embarrassed at the commotion my 'innocent
remark' had created, but then a 'eureka' moment caused the
biggest smile to erupt upon my face – *'She obviously believes I
do live up to my convictions, after all!☺'*

11. Blessed Be God! How Wonderful Are His Ways!

As we entered the 'Festive Season', I had mixed feelings as I looked back at my first Christmas in Brighton – a celebration in which everything from the Christmas play to Christmas cakes to Christmas gifts began with promise but 'flopped' at the end. This year there was no mention of a Christmas play, but the previous year Sister Stevie both wrote and directed a nativity play. A number of older Sisters willingly volunteered to play a part, while the postulants simply followed orders! Yvonne was to play Joseph and I, with my fat baby face, was to be the shepherd boy who having no gift to present to the Baby King would play a tune on a flute for him. The problem with that plan was I didn't have a musical gift either! In rehearsals, I might achieve success three times out of ten, usually when the whole cast hummed the tune. What a pity they didn't do so in the final play, presented not only to the Sisters in Brighton, but also to the leadership from the Mother House. My face turned from red to purple as I attempted for the third time to play a tune for the little King Jesus. Everyone laughed as Sister Aiden, the senior shepherd, unable to take the embarrassment any longer, pushed me out the stable door!

I was working in the kitchen at the time. In theory, with A Level Domestic Science behind me, I should be successful in that domain! Penny took time to find out my strengths and let me work in those areas – all to do with sweetness – cakes, biscuits, scones, and even decorating cakes. My enthusiasm, however, was not enough to create a smooth run. One of my first tasks was to bake fruit scones. With an inward pride, I prepared them from scratch without looking at a recipe book. I then put them in the oven and went off to the chapel to pray, returning to a furious Penny, holding a tray of charcoaled bakes.

'Where have you been? They're ruined! What do you t'ink you're doing, just leaving dem?'

'I thought they took 30 minutes.'

'10 minutes – 10 minutes, dat's all they take. If you didn't know you should have asked!'

Penny looked up at the clock, 'You'll have to start again – and be quick; you can't be late for your lesson!'

I went to the small room set aside for baking, upset but determined to get it right this time! After a while, Penny's full-time assistant, Sister 'Attie, bounded in. She hadn't seen a need for me to work in the kitchen, taking some of her jobs, so as she entered I cringed on the inside, expecting a rebuke, but she surprised me!

'Don't worry, luv, we all got 'o learn. I've finished me work now; do you want some help?'

I smiled back, 'Yes, please!'

In no time at all, 'Attie, built like a tank and faster than a whirlwind, threw the trays into the waiting oven and clapped the flour from her hands, 'There, all done!'

In the afternoon, Penny, lightheartedly entered the dining room with plate in hand. 'C'mon, now', she insisted, 'everyone taste dese scones Kaitlyn made.' Laughing, and glancing over at me, she added, 'You don't know de trouble she went to, to make them!'

My biggest mistake in the kitchen happened when Penny was away. 'Attie was thrilled to be in charge, brimming to have such responsibility. Penny, before leaving, asked me to bake Scottish shortbread for St. Andrew's Day. Making extra of these delicious biscuits for later in the week, I decorated the plates with homemade Scottish flags, knowing the Scottish Sisters would appreciate this extra little gesture. *'Fanfare'*, I demanded, coming into the dining room, with large tray in hand. 'Attie and Yvonne formed a little tune, and all tucked into the shortbread – only to cover their mouths with hands and serviettes, except for 'Attie that is. The demand for British middle-class behaviour had no effect on her. She spat the shortbread out of her mouth and as it fell to the floor blurted out in her broad Lancashire accent, 'Ahh . . . that's full o' salt.'

I ran to the baking-room and dipped my finger into the sugar container – *'It's salt!'*

'Attie, eager to keep the kitchen 'ship-shape' while in charge realised she was at fault. 'Sorry, luv, I must 'av' poured salt in by mistake.'

My face was scarlet, and although not at fault, I was far too embarrassed to re-enter the dining room, finding washing-up that 'needed' my attention. 'Attie threw the homemade short-bread in the bin and Sister Celia replaced it with a box of bought shortbread.

After that, I was mostly a success in the kitchen. Having talked about my hobby of making novelty cakes for my family, Penny set me the unenviable challenge of decorating 26 Christmas cakes. I enthusiastically began by designing intricate icing-pictures – copying from Christmas cards, I planned to present 26 unique cakes to *'wow'* the Sisters, creating outlines of characters and objects in thick icing before filling the shapes with appropriately coloured thin icing. I even spent what free-time I had down in the cellar continuing my work, but after a month I knew I had to simplify the designs if I was to complete the task in time, pouring icing onto the last few cakes and splatting it with a spatula to create a snow-scene! In the early days, however, the elderly Sisters would receive a detailed account of the complex pictures I had 'painted' on the cakes.

'We will all have opportunity to appreciate your hard work this afternoon', Sister Juliet informed me at lunchtime on Christmas Eve. 'We'll be having Christmas cake with our afternoon tea.'

'Really?'

'Yes, I'm looking forward to seeing your creations – they sound fascinating!'

I kept an eye on the time all afternoon, ready to race across to the main-house at 3.30p.m. to be with the Sisters for the unveiling of my masterpiece. As I ran, I excitedly wondered which of the cakes Penny would reveal, picturing the two Santas shaking hands, the penguin on skis, even the air-brush winter scene with Robin taking centre-stage – surely 'good enough to be framed'! Entering the dining room, I scanned the area to find 'the best seat in the house'! Sisters Aiden and Juliet were sitting together – perfect – being the most articulate of Sisters, they would discuss the intricate detail for half-an-hour! And Sisters Roisin and Dorcas sitting with them – this gathering must be arranged by God, for only praise comes out of their mouths! Quietly sitting by Sister Dorcas, smiling as always, was Sister Lucy who, hardly able to see the cake, would customarily join in with an enthusiastic *'woo'*!

As I joined the small gathering, Sister Aiden opened the conversation. 'So, Katey, today we get to see the wonderful creations we've heard so much about.'

I beamed! If the old Sisters were like Grannies, Sister Aiden was 'Number 1 Granny'; I revelled in her praise. In comes Penny, casual as you like, cake in hand – Fanfare from Sisters Aaron and Roisin – the cake is place on the table – silence! Jaws drop . . . Bewildered looks upon faces . . . My greatest supporters are speechless! Of the 26 Christmas cakes I embellished, the worst of the batch sits before us – if it had been a kitten, it would have been the runt of the litter! – the very last cake I decorated. With hardly enough icing left in the bowl, I had decided to 'spread it thin' rather than make up more icing. I looked up from the pitiful sight before us – 'Penny, where are the others I decorated?'

'Oh, I gave dose away as gifts', Penny answered in a matter-of-fact fashion, as she headed back toward the kitchen. 'You can slice the cake.'

Gutted, I sliced and delivered cake amidst voices of encouragement –

'Never mind.'

'I'm sure it will be delicious!'

'Just think how blessed the postman will be.'

'And the milkman . . . even the butcher!'

At least no one reminded me of the adage, 'Pride goes before a fall'!

Earlier in December, on a beautifully crisp afternoon, everything glistening in the snow, Yvonne and I, still in freedom as postulants, had decided to build a snowman outside the dining room to surprise the elderly Sisters after their naps. The idea came to me as I remembered a night I spent on sleepover duty with Sr. Bernice, a high-spirited, Irish middly, in charge of one of the Children's Homes in Chester. 1.30a.m. and the two of us were still up sharing stories, eating our way through a tin of Roses chocolates, when snow suddenly began to fall thick and fast. Initially standing at the dining room window, as excited as any child by this first fall of snow, Bernice soon enthused, 'C'mon, we should go build a snowman – surprise d' children when they wake up in d' morning!'

Sure enough, the children could hardly contain their excitement when they saw a fully clad snowman, with not only scarf, gloves and hat, but even wellies, smiling back at them. They never gobbled down breakfast so quickly, before racing to put on their coats, but with Sr. Bernice over at the Convent, the staff-in-charge refused their requests to go out to play.

'If you fall over, you'll get all wet, and then we'll have to change you before school.'

As the children whined at her decision, a high-speed, blue-veiled nun skidded past the kitchen window, the door flew open and an Irish lilt rang out, 'C'mon children, come out to play. I've made youse a slide already.'

Cheers rose up as the young children raced into the garden, squeals of laughter soon ringing throughout the neighbourhood, none more childlike than Sr. Bernice's!☺

In our situation, just as Yvonne and I were placing the snowman's head on its shoulders, the Convent car sheepishly returned from an outing. Heading toward the garage, three middlies sat within and gave a wave in our direction. We returned the wave and then smiled at one another; with the same thought, we needed no further communication. We raced to the side of the garage and began forming ammunition as the Sisters unloaded the car. As they appeared, we began throwing our missiles. To our surprise, both Sisters Celia and Penny dropped the bags and retaliated. Wow! We were having a snowball fight! Maggie-May, on the other hand, waved her hands full of shopping bags profusely as she skidded across to the hedge, heading for the Main House, squealing in her delightfully high-pitched Cork accent, *'Ahh! No!'* It was almost more fun to aim the snowballs at her than at the two willing to play, but Penny especially was a good shot, so it was important to keep an eye on her! After a few shots, I needed to make more snowballs. I should never have turned my back on our opponents! As I was reaching down to the ground, the Sisters ran at me, Celia pulling the collar of my coat and Penny dropping a big dollop of snow down my back.

'Game over!' Celia declared, brushing the snow from her leather gloves.

Both Sisters picked up their bags triumphantly as I ran to Yvonne, begging her to remove the snow while I imitated an Indian rain dancer! It was not easy to admit defeat, but now the competition had begun, Yvonne and I would have no problem finding ingenious ways to get them back! Meanwhile, our attention turned to all those bags the Sisters carried in to the main-house – Christmas Presents! We followed the Sisters into the office in the hope of taking a peek. The bags sat unguarded in the corner. Looking up at the clock, Yvonne casually remarked, 'Almost time for the tuck-shop. We'll man the shop for you if you want to go get a cuppa. You've had a busy afternoon.'

Sister Celia thanked us. As we calmly set out the table with chocolate bars, sweets, and crisps, inside we were laughing; any minute now we'd get to raid the bags; we'd be able to guess everyone's gifts, even our own! Celia just as calmly unlocked the cupboard before her, and in no time at all every bag had disappeared behind lock and key. Looking at our disappointed faces, Sister Celia, with laughing eyes, managed to keep a straight face.

'Very kind of you to offer to do the tuck-shop!'

Celia hummed a tune as she headed toward the kitchen and we were aware she had beaten us again!

When Christmas day arrived, Sister Celia played Father Christmas, in as far as she reached inside the sack and called out the name on the gift. Meanwhile, her little helpers, Penny and Christine, collected the sacks from the office and Maggie-May handed the gifts to the excited recipients. Everyone got at least two gifts, except for the postulants, receiving only one. Yvonne, at least, got something she wanted – fresh ink for her calligraphy art. I, on the other hand, got a Parker pen. I put this down to lack of knowledge; you don't know what to buy someone, buy them a pen! I felt rejected and upset. Yvonne and I quickly left the party. As we passed Sister Aiden, she was opening the larger of her two gifts – a beautiful Aran cardigan.

'Look, Sisters, at my beautiful gift . . . what did you get?'

Without stopping, I waved my gift ungratefully toward her – 'A pen!'

Funnily enough, I would love such a gift now, but only seeing rejection in it then, I decided as I reached my second Christmas I would not hope for anything I might appreciate. Mum would be arriving on the 29th. She would bring gifts from home; gifts bought especially for me! When Christmas day arrived, however, I felt very much appreciated by the Sisters. Yet, for all of us, there was a concern much greater than material possessions. On Christmas Eve, the whole convent was so sad when informed Sister Avril the night before had suffered an extremely serious stroke, and appeared to lose her mind, becoming uncontrollably violent. Strapped to a bed to keep her safe, she had only the Christmas holidays to improve or she would be admitted to a psychiatric ward. Everyone was devastated by this news, but only Filis and I felt such a move was unjust, having nurses within our own 'family' who were able to take care of her. I was concerned not only for Sister Avril, but for all the elderly Sisters who, in seeing Avril carted off, would live in fear of similar rejection. As Olive Oil said to me many times, Sister Filis and I were in the age of idealism – and that meant our opinions had no validity!

I hope we carry our ideals into the future. When we are the 'middlies' making the decisions, I hope we say, 'Our Sisters come first – through taking care of our own, we proclaim the good Word to the nations.' Don't let us lose our convictions, Jesus, but just for now, take care of Avril. Grant her peace, Lord God!

I began to spend as much time with Sister Avril as I could. On entering the room, I would be met by a teary-eyed elderly Sister sitting by a raving Avril, frantically trying to break free from the safety harnesses around her. Whoever the Sister was, she would be glad of the replacement, quickly relinquishing the vigil seat to escape with her sadness. I, on the other hand, enjoyed being with Sister Avril – not for any sadistic reason, I might add! As soon as we were alone, I would stroke her hair while singing in tongues (a heavenly language given by the Holy Spirit through which He prays when we don't know how to). Sister Avril would be transformed immediately; the shuffling of her body to wangle free would stop, as would the shouting. Complete peace would envelop her, the only movement in her body brought about by gentle breathing while a smile as innocent as a baby's would appear on her face. Occasionally, giggles as pure as a child's laughter would bubble forth from her lips.

*Lord, it's Christmas. A friend of a little boy comes along and gives him a puppy. The boy cries in excitement, 'Please, Daddy, can we keep it?' I'm just the same. Please, Father, let us keep your daughter with us where she will receive love – the only true medicine of life. Don't let her be sent to an institution. Let us keep her, please! I place my trust in You, Lord God. Blessed be God; **how wonderful are His ways!***

When I prayed to be able to keep Sister Avril with us, my thoughts were towards God changing hearts of 'the powers that be'. I don't know whether anyone else prayed for healing, but I don't remember doing so. Yet, God answered my prayers, and the prayers of the other Sisters, with a miracle – Sister Avril woke up the day before she should be sent away, restored in mind and body. In the coming weeks, seeing her wander down to the kitchen each evening at bedtime to fill her hot water bottle was as majestic to me as the Wise Men finding the star that led them to the Baby King Jesus. While in her sickbed, I had whispered into Sister Avril's ear many times, *'God is good'* – I had believed it with all my heart, and God had proven it with all of His!

A quarter of a century later while I wait for God to fulfil His promise of using my hands for miracles, I don't pray so much to see the miracles as to share in Jesus' compassion, for again and again in the Gospels of Jesus' life, we read of His compassion transforming lives:

When Jesus saw a great multitude He was moved with *compassion* for them, and out of that compassion healed *their* sick (Matthew 14:14).

When He fed the 4,000 with only seven loaves of bread and a few fish it was out of *compassion*, recognising their hunger (Matthew 15:32).

When the two blind men asked Jesus to enable them to see, He had *compassion* on them and touched their eyes that they should see (Matthew 20:29–34).

When the leper knelt before Jesus, begging him to make him clean, Jesus moved with *compassion*, stretched out His hand and touched him, saying *'I am willing, be cleansed'* (Mark 1:40–41).

Another time, on seeing the crowd, Jesus had *compassion* on them, recognising them to be like sheep without a shepherd, and in response taught them many things (Mark 6:34). The same *compassion* makes God cry, *'My people are destroyed for lack of knowledge'* (Hosea 3:6); for His heart is that none should perish (2 Peter 3:9).

Jesus raised a man from the dead because He had *compassion* on his mother, recognising her to be a widow and this dead man, her only son. In the culture of her time, without a husband or son to provide for her, this woman would not only be lonely and sorrowful, but destitute. Jesus' *compassion* not only raised the widow's son, but also saved the life of the widow (Luke 7:11–15)!

Smith Wigglesworth, a man through whom Jesus worked many miracles in the early part of the 20th Century, would throw emotional friends and family of a sick person out of the bedroom, claiming God could not work in a room full of sympathy; compassion, not sympathy, was needed for miracles to be performed!

As I look back at the miracle Sister Avril experienced, I can't help wondering if, back then, I was inadvertently closer to sharing Jesus' compassionate heart than I am today. Later, when I cared for my Momma I could not have felt greater compassion, and wondered as I wept, if I would ever feel this depth of love for other people.

Of course, in both these cases, I was in personal relationship, and my prayers ascended from a heart filled with love. To see miracles amongst people I hardly know in the natural, I must somehow enter more deeply Christ's compassion – He who knows every detail of their lives, past, present and future, and loves the very fibre of their beings, He who longs to say 'Yes' to their request, 'Jesus, will you make me well?'

How do we love with this depth of compassion – is it a gift Jesus gives us or is it something we must learn as when Jesus says 'learn from Me'? I guess it's a little of both, but whatever it takes, I do believe having the heart, the compassion, of Jesus Christ for people will be a major key to seeing His healing power manifested in lives throughout the world in the coming days.

12. Ask and You Shall Receive

The last Sunday of the month marked an important day in the Convent Calendar, the Rescue Thanksgiving Mass. Every car filled to capacity, we sped off to Chester to join in the celebrations. In the Cathedral, I sat with Sister Marietta who had taken care of the Volunteer group and Claire, a volunteer in my year, now a member of staff. Everyone once again spoiled the one-and-only novice☺. Enjoying talking with special friends within the Sisterhood, I nonetheless felt no great pangs to stay when it was time to leave, nor the tight stomach muscles I had felt on previous occasions. I was content to return 'home', nonetheless all could see where I truly belonged. The following morning, Josepi remarked, 'I zink vwen you are professed (graduate) you vwil go to Rescue.'

'Yes, I zink so', I replied with a smile☺

Perhaps Mum's imminent arrival was part of my acceptance in returning to Brighton:

Dear Lord,   *29.12.86*

11p.m. in the Novitiate and I've just stopped talking! How's that possible? My Momma's arrived and O.O has taken on

night duty in the Infirmary. I won't be able to stay up late
chatting every night; I need to fit in prayer and sleep too,
but it's so good to be with my Momma. Thank You. ☺

Mum's five-day visit brought joy to my heart, beginning to
end. As we kissed each other goodnight on that first night, I
handed over my alarm clock and the responsibility of waking
me in the mornings. The Novitiate was on a two-week break
from studies so I hardly saw O.O while spending every free
moment with my Momma. I still did my duties in the
Infirmary. Mum would watch me with the greatest of pride
as I brought the infirm Sisters, one by one, into the chapel
each morning, hopefully no longer accused of 'plonking them
down'! As we joined the Sisters in the dining room for the
various meals each day I felt proud of her too for being
'herself', relaxed, with quick wit and a hearty laugh. One
suppertime, Mum peeled an orange in 'one move', dropping
its 'twirly coat' onto her side plate.

'I bet you can't do that!' Sister Finnian challenged me.

I had never before seen my Momma peel an orange that
way nor previously attempted it myself, but ever the competitor, I set out to prove Sister Finnian wrong.

'Da-da!' I proudly announced, holding in the air my own
'curly coat'.

On Mum's last afternoon, the two of us chatting as much
as on the night she arrived, my Novice-Mistress came into the
community room without my seeing her pass the window or
hearing the front door click; I hadn't had time to prepare for
her arrival! Shock hit my face faster than a high-speed train,
my body instantly rigid, readjusting to sit straight. Only my
voice sounded 'normal', although a little posher than Mum
was used to! Sister Peter was only with us moments, pleasantly
greeting us before disappearing into her room for the night.

My Momma looked at me perplexed and concerned. 'Why are you afraid of her? . . . You reacted like that yesterday when she came into the dining room over at the Convent. You've never been afraid of anyone!'

Mum's observation was not based totally on truth; having managed a lifetime of hiding my fears, masquerading as 'a sensitive tummy'. Now, the overwhelming anxiety I suffered daily coupled with erratic eating patterns, bouncing between fasting and gluttony, was too heavy a burden for my stomach to carry alone! Every muscle and blood cell must help in paying the toll, and that meant the truth coming to the surface – in my rigid body, although not in my tongue. Trying to speed-thaw my frozen body, I assured Mum I was still afraid of no one, casually responding, 'Mum, you worry too much! I'm fine. How's about a nice cup of tea?'

That evening before bed, my Momma presented me with my clock.

'No! You have to wake me tomorrow', I demanded, as inner panic set in.

'I don't want you to become dependent on me waking you.'(Too late, the damage is already done!)

'Mum, please, you have to wake me tomorrow', I begged.

The next morning, Mum entered my room with my small ornate gold clock with pearl face, its case the disguise of a book. A gift Momma had given me one Christmas, inside the front and back cover were photo frames, hosting pictures of my mother and deceased sister, Marion. As she handed it to me, Mum assured me of her prayers for me to wake in the mornings.

That evening, rummaging upstairs in cupboards while I waited for Sister Lucy to complete her duties on the throne, I found a duvet. Obviously, no one was using it. I would sneak it into the Novitiate for the remainder of my time there, hoping with a lighter covering than the blankets provided I would sleep more lightly, thus ending my struggle to wake in the mornings. Sorted!

The only sadness from Mum's visit was her news of troubles at home, troubles that burdened an already heavy heart! While most family members were 'doing ok', some seemed to be travelling a downward spiral:

Deep down it hurts that I don't see progress but regression
and, Oh Lord, so very much aggression! I wonder why
You're not showing Yourself to be answering my prayers! Yet,
at the same time, I trust and hope in You. Those qualities,
my Lord, are Your gifts, but alongside my hope is anxiety.
I wonder what will happen to them; it's all so baffling!

Well used to seeing Jesus answer my prayers, I was baffled by His 'slack hand' toward my family, but of course, God is not slack to answer our prayers, but graciously patient to wait for our willingness to receive His blessings. My whole family will have wonderful testimonies to share (and I'll be their scribe!☺) Meanwhile, Mum's observation of my relationship with my Novice-Mistress catapulted me into stark reality regarding my own situation; things were far from okay in my world too! I was consumed by fear!

I'm afraid – of failure, of punishment, of O.O more than
I trust You. I'd like to trust You with childlike faith, but
rather I'm preoccupied with that woman.

Every day I made promises to myself – promises of not speaking ill of the Novice-Mistress and of going to bed early so I could arise in time for early morning prayers – and every day I broke them! On top of my fear, hate crept back into my heart toward my Novice-Mistress. Yvonne had requested a January visit. Although Sister Celia refused her, we both concluded Olive Oil made the decision – she was against us! I felt so angry toward Olive Oil, but could say nothing to her. Bitterness, instead, took over my heart, unleashed in the main-house in a bombardment of blatant complaints about the Novice-Mistress, even shouting across to Filis one morning, *'She's so stupid!'* as a message from her was delivered. I saw such hurt in the faces of my hearers that I should speak of my superior like that – everyone knew she was not perfect, but she didn't deserve such cruel assessment. Not only that, I could see they were sad for me – 'such a lovely young Sister', they'd think, 'if only she wouldn't let her tongue ruin her!'

On top of the failings obvious to others, I also failed miserably in an area I felt a special calling from Jesus to follow. I had fasted ever since I invited Jesus into my heart. I don't remember my school-friends, who shared the same love affair with Jesus, fasting; I would walk to the local 'Chippie' with them at lunch time on Fridays, correcting my rumbling tummy for exaggerating its hunger. Anyone coming home with me for tea before the meeting in Maltby would receive a warm dinner followed by a delicious pudding while I would eat a couple of slices of freshly baked bread Mum especially bought from the bakery. By the time I entered the Convent, the habit deeply ingrained in my lifestyle, fasting not only on Fridays but on Wednesdays too, insistence was made that I *'eat something for strength'*, so I took a slice of bread for breakfast and supper, and mashed potatoes at lunchtime (my main drink was always water, so nothing changed there). This pattern of lifestyle was okay when I had a companion, but after Yvonne left, I sought comfort from food, even when I was 'fasting'. Yvonne and I both loved the crusts of bread, so we had to share them. After she was gone, one Friday morning three crusts sat in the breadbin, so I ate all three!

The worst of my gluttony occurred on Thursdays, in major panic over being sandwiched between two fast days, especially if Penny baked bread that day! I couldn't resist 'just one more slice'. One Thursday evening, skipping down the stairs after helping Lucy to bed, I stopped at the bottom. To the right was the chapel where I should attend choir practice and to the left was the kitchen where Penny's freshly baked bread lay. I turned left! Standing in the dark, munching away on thick slices of Penny's bread, as tasty as any cake, I heard footsteps coming along the corridor. The kitchen had two doors, both leading onto the corridor. I wanted to escape, but because of the echo, could not decipher the direction of the footsteps. Before I could make a decision as to which door I should run, the light switched on and Penny passed me by. I hid my utter embarrassment with a friendly, *'hello'*. Penny picked up her watch from the window-sill and dryly remarked, before walking out again, 'Eating again? You'll be spreading out into de desert!'

Lord, I was glad it was Penny who found me!

For all this gluttony, though, I was not increasing weight, but losing it, far too anxious to have food settle in my stomach before it made a hasty exit! One dinnertime, as I poured homemade blackberry jam onto my second helping of Penny's creamy rice pudding, Celia passed by to answer the phone. 'Careful, Sister Mary Kaitlyn, you don't want to look like a hippo.'

Sister Aiden scolded her, 'Sister, don't say things like that! Look at the size of her; we need to encourage her to eat, not discourage her!'

By this time, Celia was humming defiantly as she walked out the door and I was left in peace to spoon warm, creamy comfort food into my mouth. Would you like the recipe? I made a little book of all my favourite recipes – first for 45 (the number Penny was used to catering for), then we worked out the quantities for four! I guess you'll just want the quantity for four!

Penny's Creamy Rice Pudding

INGREDIENTS:
4oz (110g) pudding rice
1 pint (570ml) whole milk
14 ½ oz (410g) evaporated milk
1½oz (40g) caster sugar
1 whole nutmeg
1oz (25g) butter

DIRECTIONS:
1. Preheat oven to 150°C/300°F/gas mark 2
2. Lightly butter a 9 inch (23cm) round oven proof dish, 2 inches (5cm) deep
3. Place rice pudding and sugar in the dish
4. Mix whole milk and evaporated milk together, then pour into dish
5. Grate nutmeg onto pudding ingredients, dotting the butter on top
6. Put in the oven for 30 minutes, then take out and stir (do the same 30 minutes later)
7. Return the pudding to the oven for another hour without stirring
8. Serve warm with jam or stewed fruit (yum, yum!☺)

I could divert my attention to such things as Penny's yummy food, as I've just done now, yet, inside there was continuous turmoil, a world-war taking residence in my stomach! The New Year celebrations over, it was time for Novitiate classes to return to 'normal'. I dreaded my first lessons with O.O, writing to Jesus minutes before we should meet in the community room:

I'm justified in fearing the lessons; this is when she pounces! She has many good points, many more than the bad, but she pounces on me, changing like a schizophrenic while I feel like a defenceless child. I'll never be able to trust her no matter how nice she might behave toward me! If my emotions were read on a temperature chart, it would reach 105 degrees easily! There's no way anyone can think sensibly when in that state. I won't be able to find a solution until I calm down. I can't calm myself down. Are You going to do it, Lord?

I tried to find 'escape' in many ways, indoors as well as out. I enjoyed a number of hobbies – painting and drawing, knitting and sewing, card-making and guitar-playing, not forgetting cycling, of course! Sister Stevie insisted, in later years, when I take on the responsibility of full-time work, I would not be able to continue this large range of hobbies. I totally disagreed, and although she would not live to see it, hoped to prove her wrong. So-o-o-o! If decades later, social-analysts arrived at my door to make a final assessment, what would be the conclusion of this debate? How many of these Novitiate-based hobbies do I continue today? Well, my painting is atrocious, drawing a forgotten art, making cards too time-consuming, I don't remember one tune on the guitar or how to make knitting needles work, I can't sew in a straight line, and I don't even own a bike! I would have to concede, Sister Stevie's observation was correct!

160

As a child, on a winter's evening, I appreciated the comfort of a warm fire awaiting my return from school. As a novice, it might take me all evening to leave my hobbies and go visit with my Lord, but once I arrived in the main-house chapel, I found comfort sitting alone, 'post-exodus' (after the oldies' 8p.m. bedtime), the main lights switched off, one small candle flickering before the large, wide iron-wrought window looking out to the blackened sky. Perhaps the sky would twinkle with stars or be completely dark; whichever it was, I would always feel welcome and comforted, sensing the calling of God to come deeper into His presence and peace. Occasionally, time would be lost in the presence of my First Love and I would suddenly hear Sister Finnian locking doors. Cinderella was about to meet trouble as the clock struck, not twelve, but ten. I would have to race up the hill to the Novitiate, avoiding a scolding for my lateness. (We were to be in our bedrooms for ten, and lights out for ten-thirty; the latter I very rarely managed, but as my Novice-Mistress never came upstairs to check, I didn't need to worry!)

I felt like 'Cinderella' in many ways, my living in Brighton likened to a 'rags-to-riches' story. I grew up in a village in which I believed, rightly or wrongly, that only one family was poorer than ours. They were obviously poorer than we were; our hand-me-down clothes were clean, their rags were filthy, and the children reportedly took their monthly bath in the swimming pool!

I told a friend once of Momma's resourcefulness during those early years, 'Mum always had ingredients for pastry so when the only other food in the pantry was a tin of beans, she made Bean Pie.'

My friend who grew up in financial security, the young owner of two ponies, was horrified – 'What? Is that it? Did she not even serve it with potatoes?'

That was the point of the story; *we didn't have any potatoes that day!* Plenty of days we did have full meals, but one Sunday when friends called on me to 'come play', Mum was at the chip pan, feeding her brood of six, and a few more as the twins, Johnny and Marion, ten years my senior, always had friends visiting. Years later, the twins' friends thanked Momma for her big heart, *'feeding the village'* with plates-full of her famously tasty, chunky chips, yet, my play-'mates' made me feel so ashamed for being *'too poor to have a "proper" Sunday dinner'*! At least we lived in a nice-enough village then, but later, when Momma and I needed to escape her second marriage, the only house she could find was in the infamously poorest area of a nearby town. Now, ironically, in promising to live the vow of poverty, I lived in luxury!

I enjoyed exploring Brighton Hall from the moment Sister Alison took me, along with the rest of the Volunteers, on a tour of the House. As a postulant and novice, sitting on the bay window of the Long Room was one of my favourite 'time alone' spots, enjoying the oak panelling and elegant light-fittings to suit the Tudor period it was built in, as well as a gigantic banqueting table, conjuring up exciting scenarios of centuries' past exquisite Banquets and Balls. In the evenings, the Sisters informed me, my belly-laughter beginning its journey in the kitchen, travelled up three floors to the rafters of the Long Room, branching off through closed doors into their 'closets'. In the afternoons, loving my privacy, I could silently pass by taking comfort from being unseen and non-judged. Books in the library, some of which were over a hundred years old, on floor-to-ceiling shelves, sparked lively debate within my mind as if the authors were right there in the room with me. From the rooftop, I may be satisfied with the magnificent view of the countryside or, seeing the potential for a helicopter pad in the spacious grounds, I'd take an imaginary flight.

I don't suppose my 'flights of fancy' were anything like you suspect. My dreams would head into my future, far beyond the Novitiate walls into my destiny as revealed by God. In my dreams, I would achieve flight by living up to my convictions as seen in the lives of recent great heroes such as Gandhi, Mother Theresa and Nelson Mandela. Yet, I also dreamt of walking in the footsteps of 'role models' closer to home – my Sisters! I dreamt of being as good a House-Mother as Bernice, creating 'home from home' for the children in her care, to be as caring and dedicated a Social Worker as Jean, and to affect hundreds of young lives in Kenya as Angelina had done in her teaching and Novice-Mistress role in East Africa. I loved much about my life in Brighton – the beautiful countryside, loving relationships with many of the Sisters and the incredible opportunity to spend time alone with Jesus, but when all that was not enough, dreaming of my future was one method that helped me to cope. January, however, brought the 'blues' in stronger force than any gale. In this, my 'winter of discontent', all my mental escapes were not enough!

The third successive death occurring in the Infirmary in as many weeks greatly compounded my fears. I could hardly understand my emotions, but I knew they were related to loss – loss of life, loss of relationships, and loss of hope! On the night of Sister Eugene's death, I was unable to sleep, praying for assurance that she was okay, eventually picking up my Bible, asking Jesus for a word confirming her place in Heaven. God never fails! I was so appreciative of His speedy assurance as I read,

Then the curtain hanging in the Temple was torn in two . . .
God's people who had died were raised to life.

(Matthew 27:51, 53 GNB)

The following morning I slept in again, my latest lie-in yet, arising at an unbelievable 7.25a.m. Rushing out onto the landing, Sister Stevie met me, chuckling, 'We've finished', before disappearing into her bedroom. All the retired Sisters made light of my constant lateness, be it for prayers or meals, nicknaming me 'the Late Sister Mary Kaitlyn'. Novice-Mistresses have to be a lot more serious though! Quickly appearing, Olive Oil stared at me with a face purple with fury. My apology, 'I just can't believe it', was met by austere words – 'I can!'

Olive Oil then began to rant at me, 'Do you think I like getting up at 5.30a.m.?' sounding more like a wife who had been up all night with the baby while her husband slept through all the crying. She even criticised my being able to enjoy God's presence in my waking hours! 'Wait until you're my age and you're constantly met by a brass heaven!'

In the evening, when I thought about her comment, I felt sad for her! I will never be met by her brass heaven because I have the Spirit of Jesus Christ living inside me. I wished I could explain the importance of inviting Jesus into one's heart and receiving the infilling of the Holy Spirit so she could go beyond her prayers and rituals to hear the voice of God and feel His closeness, but I was too nervous in her company to ever hope to communicate God's immeasurable love, that doesn't depend on our 'doing', but all Christ has already accomplished on our behalf, so all I could do was pray for her. In that early morning moment outside the chapel, though, I began to cry – not tears of emotion; I was not yet conscious enough for emotion! These were tears of tiredness, but my Novice-Mistress obviously read it as the former. Relief, even a small smile, came to her face.

'Cracked her at last', I could hear her inner thoughts proclaim.

There were no excuses for my lying-in, especially as she had told me I could ask her or Sister Stevie to wake me. Shocked by this statement, I asked, 'When did you say that?'

'I said it's a pity you don't have another novice to wake you.'

Crazy woman and her ridiculous implications! Anyway, from now on, I'll be motivated to be up at 6a.m. At 6.15, she's coming to wake me! I want to be in the bathroom by then!

The following morning I was up, washed and dressed, sitting in the Chapel at 5.45a.m. January 13th marked the day for our little 'community' to discuss the Pink Paper on 'Concept of Religious Life'. I rebuked myself as I walked down the stairs to join the Sisters in the community room; if I get any backlash from this, it's my own stupid fault! I should not have prayed in tongues for half-an-hour before looking at the questions. I should have just written my own quick answers instead of relying on Holy Spirit! For this meeting, though, I had a plan – no more stuttering! As soon as I was asked to share 'my' insights, I sped through the answers. Stevie stopped writing, unable to keep up. Both Sisters leaned forward to catch more of what I was saying. Looking at my last full stop, I sighed within, *'I've finished; done it!'*

Stevie, amazed, complimented me, 'That's so good! Your insights are so full of wisdom.'

'Yes, quite remarkable', Sister Peter confirmed, 'But we couldn't catch everything – can you read it again?'

'And slowly this time', Stevie innocently added, not realising she was helping to erect my gallows!

Again, I read the sentences before me. Again, Stevie wrote nothing, giving her full attention to my every word. When I finished, they sat amazed, shaking their heads, muttering, 'So good; so good.'

Stevie was the first to ask for a complete copy of my answers, quickly followed by my Novice-Mistress. I despaired! Now, I would not be able to make one wrong move in community living without being told I did not live up to my principles! After all I'd been through, and yet my greatest failure was still ahead of me!

Within days, the snow was up to our knees (literally!) For safety's sake, Stevie was to stay in the main-house until the snow thawed. I knew it was the best solution for her, but what about me I cried! They couldn't leave me alone in the Novitiate with the Novice-Mistress! Could I not also stay in the main-house? Celia just laughed at my 'over-acting'. In the afternoon, in a bid to 'get away', I trudged to Brighton Church, and stood gazing at the sheep in the field for some time, mesmerised by their peaceful, gentle nature, accepting life as it is given to them.

I wonder what they get out of life. We get roast lamb and woolly jumpers, but what do they get?

As I returned to the Novitiate, I was dreading my first meal alone with my Novice-Mistress. Obviously, she dreaded it more than me, talking non-stop! She gave me a bulletin from 'the Passage' in London, ministering to 'down-and-outs', knowing I'd be interested in the work there.

'No reason to be running off to the Passage though,' she responded to my enthusiasm.

I had been seeking courage to ask if I could have my final placement as a novice there; this was my cue!

'It would be good experience though!'

Sister Peter went on to tell me how she had already arranged for us to visit one day in April when we would be in London for the Franciscan Novices' Meeting,

'Keep that between ourselves for now.'

I was pleased with the suggestion, but three months seemed like a lifetime. I needed a break *NOW!* I saw the solution to my bad attitude toward my Novice-Mistress and Novitiate training was a quick break from Sister Peter – on my return, I would appreciate her as I did on our last reunion. No one seemed to notice the dangerous place I was in; I was like a high-speed train about to lose control and come skidding off the track into a built-up housing estate, leaving carnage behind.

Sister Aiden had fallen off her pedestal, good and proper, sounding like a broken record, repeatedly advising me to *'just hold on'.*

I couldn't hold on any more! Action was needed! I turned to Sister Celia, as 'Superior', for help. 'Just two days, please! Arrange it for me – anywhere, it doesn't matter where and I don't care what work I do. Please!'

Celia laughed at my request,

'You've just had two weeks off from studies – that should have been break enough! You know your problem? – You're too independent, wanting to do your own thing. You're a novice, now, y'know!'

I was clinging to a cliff-edge with my fingernails; could no one see I was about to lose my grip! Sister Dorcas alone kept her favoured position. A chance meeting, not in either of our usual locations, but in the dining room, with others milling around, led Sister Dorcas to ask how I was. My answer was to burst into tears! She once again lovingly held me in her arms, speaking Jesus' love into my heart. Sister Dorcas was right; all I had was Jesus. His love had to be enough! In two days time I was to lead the Charismatic prayer meeting – from now until then I would pray for Jesus' direction, thinking only of the prayer meeting, not allowing any wayward, despairing thought to enter my head. Jesus gave me as the main focus of the meeting, the scripture,

> 'Ask, and you will receive; seek, and you will find; knock, and the door will be opened to you.'
>
> (Matthew 7:7 GNB)

Christ constantly reminded me, '*This is my meeting.*' Recognising I was willing to try any job, even tackling the work of God, I needed to find humility in being a tool in the Father's hand for what He wanted to accomplish that night, '*I am an instrument, not the Craftsman!*' Sister Finnian cut across the grain for me when she requested I pray with her for the gift of tongues.

> *It's your meeting, Lord. You want the very best for these Sisters. So many of them received what they asked for tonight. Penny said it was one of the best meetings she has ever been to. Next week, Josepi is leading. Prayer and fasting is my calling – an occasional leader, maybe, but more importantly, I'm called to be a hidden cog in the wheel. I ask the meeting next week go equally well because as you say, it's Your meeting! I also found consolation tonight– I have the Sisters and You give them great power;* **their love keeps me here!**

13. In the Multitude of My Anxieties, I Put My Trust in You

The next day, sitting in the back of the Convent four-door car, I felt as if I was travelling in one of those white-armoured vans with miniature, high windows, a convict returning to prison after appearing in court. Sister Peter and I together with Sister Alison were on our way back from our first day of the New Year at College. The Principal had found us in the corridor awaiting our first lecture, wanting to inform my Novice-Mistress of the change to the Course Programme – was she still interested in us attending? Even before he explained the new programme, she was quick to inform him we were not interested! Truth be told, Olive Oil had never been interested! Taking advantage of Mother Anastasia being on a plane to Holland, she swiftly took authority in making the decision alone. I was numb from the shock; how was I going to survive the monotony of Novitiate life without these twice-weekly interludes?

I'm trying to believe in divine providence, Lord – claiming nothing can happen to me that You do not allow! I feel no contemporary novice is having it as bad as me and no

Novice-Mistress is living in the past as much as mine. While other novices would not be more independent, I believe they would be more responsible. Training today is very much responsibility orientated, but not with O.O; my responsibility is to act only with her permission! I love being in the main-house as much as I am. I see a need and I attend to it. I feel free; I can be me! Whatever Your plans, don't change that, please!

The next afternoon, as I ascended the small hill to the Novitiate from the main-house, I thought on the little fantasy my mind had occasionally visited in which I escaped on the convent bike, not as I had done many times before for a few hours in an afternoon, but cycling all the way to the city and jumping on a train to go home! The image always brought a smile to my face and was enough to lift my spirit – the adventure of it; nothing more than fiction I might one day write in a novel! Once in the Novitiate, the house seemed more foreboding than only the day before when the College Principal had inadvertently played against me the 'Monopoly' game-card 'GO TO JAIL'. In the lesson O.O began, 'Just to reiterate – Monday will be our last day at College.'

Inside I cried powerlessly, *'Don't remind me'*, but sat silently, beyond sad; totally devastated!

'And while we're on the subject, during your free time, I don't want you spending time with the young Sisters' (Filis and Penny, almost 40!) 'You can spend your time in prayer.'

It was as if my brain snapped in two, a dual-cast taking centre-stage, speaking in the round. The one half never giving up on angrily asserting, *'I'm leaving, I'm leaving!'* while the other half calmly answers theoretical questions on Franciscan dogma, every answer receiving a nod of approval. (*Too late, I'm out of here!*)

As soon as the lesson was over, I completed my Saturday chores, giving the chrome in the kitchen its last buffing to make it shine and headed towards my bedroom, changing into my tracksuit, before turning to the box in which I had left my savings of £10. Not finding it, I searched all the other places I might have put it. Still I couldn't find it. I would leave without it! When I reached this place of desperation before I always did one of three things. One option was to talk to Sister Aiden but I didn't want to hear that all would be okay once I got professed – I needed my life to be okay now! My other two options hitherto employed were to pray or write in my journal, both of which persuaded me God wanted me to stay. Today I shouted to God (*quietly* so my Novice-Mistress would not hear me!) *'I'm not doing any of those things. I'm leaving!'*

I took the back of an A4 writing pad and drew a big pink smiley face with the words *'Bye! Bye!'* plastered across the top of it. I then went over to the convent and asked Filis if she could lend me £10. From here on began a lot of lies to get me home ('desperation' is no excuse, but my need to escape did become all-consuming!). As Sister Alison shopped locally on Saturdays, I said I asked her to buy something, costing £10. Asking this amount from Filis, I explained the money was in my room somewhere and as soon as I found it she could have her £10 back (that bit was true!). Filis took £55 out of her drawer, asking was I sure £10 was enough. I would have loved to take more but I only had £10 in my room so I said that was plenty! As I headed for the outside door, a couple of older Sisters passed me and greeted me cheerfully, 'Have you been cycling this afternoon?'

'Yes', I replied. I mean, I couldn't tell them I was about to borrow the convent bike and take it home to Yorkshire with me, now, could I! Being late afternoon in January, as soon as I began cycling I realised it would soon be dark. My plan was to go to the train station but that was thirteen miles away. How would I see without bike lights? A priest from a neighbouring village came to Sunday dinner every second week. I didn't know him very well but he looked the type to ride a push-bike. I would pay him a visit on my way home! Of course, I couldn't tell him the truth either, so I told him I was out on an errand; did he have any bike lights I could borrow? He offered to give me a lift if I would wait a short time. No, really, I needed to be on my way! Not having any bicycle lights, he offered to attach two torches to my bike. As he headed towards the outside door with all he required for the task I looked up at the clock – 4.45p.m. Prayers would be in fifteen minutes and I would be responsible for holding up communal prayers.

'Can I use your phone please; let the Sisters know what's happening?'

Sister Aiden (of all people!) answered the phone. In trying to cover up my Yorkshire accent I put on an Irish accent when asking for Penny. Of course, my disguise was foiled as Sister Aiden was well used to hearing K-K-Katey put on an Irish accent, but she complied with my request. I intended to tell Penny the truth, but just as she picked up the phone, the priest came in, pushing the bike along – 'It's getting dark out there. I'll do it in here.'

Time to talk in code! Penny called my Novice-Mistress by the nickname, 'Auntie Elena', so I began, 'Hi, it's Katey. Could you let Auntie Elena know I'm on my way?'

'On your way, on your way . . . what do you mean, on your way? On your way where? . . . Oh, you're never leaving!'

'That's right', I answered cheerfully, as if she had just won a magnificent prize.

Penny spoke anxiously, trying to work out my where-abouts. 'Are you over at the novitiate? Oh, you can't be – you can't ring out. Where are you? Oh, please don't go. Come back!'

I wanted to go back just to relieve Penny's distress, but I looked up at the clock. Impossible for me to be back in time for evening prayers; I feared being *'marmalade'* for being late.

'So, if you could pass that message on' I said in an outlandishly cheerful voice, 'talk to you later. Bye.'

I turned to the triumphant priest and the illuminated convent bike; everything was in order for the next leg of my journey. As I jumped on the bike, I promised Father he would have his torches back in due time. There was still enough daylight for me to make my way along the winding country roads without the aid of the torches. Having successfully arrived on the main road, the sign for Stratford-upon-Avon before me, I switched on the two lights.

'I've got us this far', I told Jesus. 'Now You'll have to get me the rest of the way home.'

Thank God for His grace toward us for I know if judgement was greater than mercy my presumptuous comment would have caused a bolt of lightning to strike me from heaven! Instead, with the first push of the pedals, the front light switched off and the back light fell to the ground. I got off the bike, picked up the fallen torch and with my nose pointing up to Heaven, shouted, *'I'm **still** going!'*

I walked towards my destination, but I still had another twelve miles to go! Up ahead, I saw a garage-cum-grocery store. I asked the owners where the nearest Police Station was. They pointed left and said 'twelve miles that way'. I asked if I could use the phone to ring the Police. I was led to the stockroom at the back of the building where an old-fashioned shiny red phone sat on the shelf. Their inquisitiveness got the better of them, sending in an assistant and a friend to 'look for something' while I spoke to the policeman on duty. I explained I desperately needed to get home but was a number of miles from the train station and only had money for the train journey. He said there were two reasons he couldn't help; firstly, being the only person on duty he wasn't to leave the desk, and secondly, he only had a pushbike himself! He suggested I get a lift from someone buying petrol.

With my captive audience hovering around me in the stockroom I put on a performance, feigning shock, 'You'll be investigating my murder in the morning giving me such advice!'

The policeman apologised and suggested I ask the owners of the garage, John and Mary, for help. Seeking their help, I found them just outside the door at two archaic cutting machines. John was cutting meat and his wife, Mary, cutting bread. Presumably someone had ordered a sandwich, but the more I asked for their help the more their heads went down, until finally Mary lifted her head and ordered her husband, 'Get the van out and get young Steve to take her to the train station.'

'Young Steve', the friend who had been hovering in the stockroom, objected strongly. 'I've got the kids tonight. I've got to pick them up at seven.'

'You'll be back before then', Mary insisted.

I was so relieved to see the bike pushed in the back of the little van before jumping in the front seat – I was on my way again! But I had a fear of being caught out and taken back to the convent, like I was an escapee 'nut' rather than trainee nun, so when I was asked what I was doing in the Cotswolds, I began another set of lies.

'My friend's dad owns a bakery in town. He gave me a job.'

'Long way to travel for a job in a bakery', he replied.

Steve then asked me was it the one at the top of Market Street.

Instead of saying 'Yes', I made a mistake. 'No', I replied, 'the one at the bottom.'

I had only been into town once. I didn't have a clue where there was a bakery or indeed if there was more than one, but Steve would know! I needed to think quickly. 'So, you're having the kids tonight – does that mean you're divorced?'

'Yes', he replied and complained for the rest of the journey about his ex-wife!

At the train station, I bought my one-way ticket to Rotherham and with less than £2 change in my pocket, climbed the stairs to the platform on the opposite side of the train tracks. While sitting on a bench in my tracksuit and cagoule, cold and damp, never taking my eyes off the entrance, I strung a couple of psalm verses together, attempting to calm my soul, 'Whenever I am afraid – in the multitude of my anxieties – I will trust in You'.[1]

The multitude of my anxieties came in the form of flying nuns. They fly through the doors of the station at top-speed, straight through the waiting room onto the platform; their bodies perfectly horizontal, hovering like bees, three Blue Nuns, flying in to take me back. Below their long waving veils, foxes' faces protrude with eyes bouncing back-and-forth on springs. As the two on either side scan the platform up and down, the central figure, the leader, glares across the railway track – she's spotted me! Her eyes spring out of their sockets, almost touching me as they bounce across the track to the platform on which I sit.

'Oh, God, in the multitude of my anxieties I will trust in You! **Bring the train, quick!'**[2]

---

[1] From Psalms 56:3 and 94:19

[2] **Footnote of Fairness**: Some Sisters would like to remind Katey she could have asked to leave and would have received a lift to the train station! Others recognise Katey's way of leaving much better suited her dramatic character!☺

Of course, following the story so far, you will know most of the Sisters are actually very nice people. My fear was not based on them being 'nasty' but that they could persuade me to go back. My relief was off the Richter scale when the train arrived to take me to Birmingham. Changing trains meant lugging the bike up and down another set of stairs to get to yet another platform. The train to Rotherham was made up of old carriages seating up to eight people. The bike safely in the luggage-cage, I went along the corridor to find myself a seat. As I sat nervously rehearsing what I might tell my Momma, the door burst open and a girl bounced in, imitating a kangaroo, 'Can I sit here?' she asked. 'I'm a born-again Christian.'

'*Good*', I thought. '*I'll try out my story on you!*' I told her everything I had done, concluding, 'I'm dreading telling my Mum.'

'I don't blame you', she replied. 'She's going to kill you!'

When I arrived in Rotherham, I couldn't travel on the bus because I had a bike to take care of. It was late and I was too tired to walk. There was only one thing I could do; I would have to use the remainder of my £10 on a taxi journey. The taxi-driver tried every which way to get that bike into his car, but it just wouldn't fit!

'Tell you what; I'm good friends with the station attendants. They'll look after your bike and you can pick it up tomorrow.'

He asked what I had been doing and I said I'd been cycling in the Cotswolds (I didn't lie!). I asked him to throw me out when my money was spent. As we passed a bus, I wanted to kick myself as I realised the reason I was in the taxi using up the last of all my wealth in the world was to transport a bike I'd left behind at the train station! The taxi-driver also liked cycling so we chatted about nice places we had each cycled. The meter showed that I'd travelled beyond my limit, but he kindly said he'd take me all the way home. When I walked in the door of the kitchen Momma came from the living room to see who had arrived. Looking at me standing aloof in front of the fridge, her Irish lilt rang out, 'Kaitlyn, you're home!'

'Yes' I replied.

'Who's wit' you?' Mum asked, peering out the window.

'No one.'

Glancing down to my feet before her head slowly lifted, her eyes meeting mine, 'Where's your luggage?'

'I don't have any.'

'Oh, you've never ran away', she remarked sympathetically before walking toward me, enveloping me in a big hug.

Momma had always found a telephone in the home an intrusion, so when living alone, had disconnected the phone (which turned out to be good because if she had a phone, presumably the Sisters would have rung to see if I was there and would have put my Momma into anxiety over my whereabouts). Borrowing money, I went to the phone-box up the road to tell the Sisters I had arrived safely. Apparently, Sisters Celia, Maggie-May, Penny and Filis sat on high stools around the large chrome kitchen tables drinking endless cups of tea, still in shock, watching the cordless phone, willing it to ring. Filis had been corrected for not telling Sisters Celia and Peter of my plan to run away – she wasn't believed when she said she knew nothing of my plan. (And it never crossed my mind that in borrowing money from her she should ever be held partly responsible!)

The moment Sister Celia answer my call, she screamed down the phone, 'Get yourself back here, *Now!*'

Through gritted teeth, I answered furiously, 'Even if I had the money and even if trains were working at this time of night, do you seriously think I've left just to travel back again?'

Celia was as confused as everyone else about my sudden departure (hadn't I been talking about my profession [graduation] only the day before!) Again, she demanded, 'Get yourself back here!'

This phone call was going nowhere! I abruptly ended the call. 'I've rung to tell you I'm home safe. I've told you, so goodnight!'

My second call, to Sister Caris in Chester, was as calm as the first call was fraught.

'Where are you?' she 'casually' asked.

'I'm at home.'

'Seriously', she asked, for some reason thinking I was joking, 'Where are you? I know you're on your way here or on your way back.'

'I've run away and I'm at home!' I answered, never sounding so deadly serious in my life as it hit me what I had done – I really had run away!

Apparently, another Sister approached the corridor in which Sister Caris stood speaking to me so, with hopes of sneaking me back into the Novitiate before anyone outside Brighton heard of my escapade, Sister Caris attempted to quickly end the call. 'Go home, have a warm bath, a good night's sleep, and ring me in the morning.'

'I'm hungry', I whinged like a young child.

'Go home, have supper, have a warm bath, a good night's sleep, and ring me in the morning.'

'OK', I smiled down the phone. 'Goodnight!'

There was no slumber for my eyes that night, however! During winter, my bedroom in the attic was too cold to sleep in so I would sleep in one of the twin beds in Momma's bedroom. Asking her to pray with me, we lay in the dark, praying and praying – and then praying some more! At about 2a.m. Mum said, 'You'll have to pray by yourself now!'

In seconds, Momma was sleeping soundly, and I was left with my thoughts. What had I done? My brain almost exploded with fear of all the rejection and rebuffs I would suffer. The next morning I rang Sister Caris who had spoken with Mother Anastasia visiting Holland. She had told her to invite me to Chester for me to share what happened. I immediately wanted to go, but of course, Mum would have to pay my train fare. She was most put out, giving me the money, but still complaining, 'Last night, you said you ran away because you wanted to come home. Now you want to go back again!'

'I don't want to go back. I want to go to Chester to see Sister Caris.'

'The Convent' was 'the Convent' as far as Momma was concerned, so my explanation just left her baffled! I travelled to Chester to spend three days with Sister Caris – or should I say nights as her day-job in the Children's Rescue office, plus her 24-hour job of running a convent, meant she must listen to the woes of the runaway novice after 10p.m.! I was housed in the 'Flat' attached to the Convent, which usually hosted visiting priests, to offer me privacy. Sister Caris was the person I had most trusted in my whole life with thoughts and feelings, but as one woman remarked at the first Charismatic Conference I attended, 'You seem to say a lot, but never really share anything of yourself.'

Up until her frighteningly accurate observation, I was happy to join the discussion groups; afterwards I chose to play basketball at 'discussion time' instead! Now I needed to talk from deep within, trying to unravel the mess I had created. It was easy to share the things that happened in the Novitiate and the way it made me feel, but to share the fears it evoked was more difficult because I knew then would come the question, *'Why do you have those fears?'*

I once commented to Mum that my childhood had been tough. She was shocked by this admittance and offended by the implication that she had been 'a bad mother'. This was not my viewpoint! In my eyes, we had been victims together. I appreciated her total commitment and steadfast love toward her family. Yet no matter what was going on in her life, Momma consistently presented to the world the picture of 'Jolly Mary', often reciting, 'Smile and the world smiles with you. Weep and you weep alone'. I behaved just like her, keeping the shedding of the tears of a clown till no-one was around. I was desperate to share my past, to unburden myself with someone I could trust, but would I betray my Momma's inferred training in now sharing painful memories with Sister Caris? For the first night at least, I chose to keep to the 'surface details' of living with Olive Oil and my own failings.

There were many characteristics I liked about Sister Caris, not least her fairness. As much as she expressed empathy for me, she never took sides against O.O, even speaking on her behalf when it seemed appropriate. I equally appreciated this quality in my Momma. I remember hearing a conversation between Mum and one of my sisters-in-law. Whilst Sally ranted and raved about something a friend had said, Mum advised, 'You need to see it from her point of view.'

Sally greatly annoyed, responded, 'And you need to stop being so "fair" all the time!'

I see this quality of 'fairness' very much needed in counselling in the body of Christ because without it we will never foster the unity Christ told us to adopt through loving one another as Christ loves us. Within our many topics that night, we spoke of the call to love, Sister Caris asserting a view I had heard her share many times before – 'You can't love others until you love yourself!'

She said it from a desire to lead me into self-love, but the words processed in my mind brought about a very different message! For the first time, I dared to share the views from the inside, the hopelessness those words evoked.

Weeping, I shared, 'I don't love myself. You're saying the love I think I have for you, for my Mum, for my family – none of it is real because I don't love myself! There's no hope for me! I hate myself! And I fear others will hate me too. I'm so afraid of rejection! I'm frightened of being with people and them seeing the real "me" because then, they'll reject me!'

Sister Caris was shocked by this admittance. 'You always appear so confident in social settings – cocky confident in fact', she added, her thoughts vocalised on a bed of gentle laughter.

'I know – it's all an act. What else can I do! I don't know who I am, so how can I "be me", accept me or love me?'

'Jesus is going to show you who you are and He will teach you to love yourself!' Squeezing my arm, she assured me, 'There's so much to love!'

On the second night, the child within was screaming, desperate to share with an understanding, caring adult of events locked away in the subconscious until Olive Oil had unwittingly poked at them, sending the child within into frightened flight. Nightmare after nightmare, shame and fear would return to haunt me. Tonight, an overwhelming sense of hopelessness was in the process of squeezing the life out of me as Sister Caris knocked on the door; I must share my story before I am swallowed into the black hole of 'no return'. In my life, no revelation would ever prove harder to expose than on this night, no emotion harder to express! Held in Sister Caris's arms, assured of acceptance, tears flowing and tissues filling, I searched desperately to find the words to begin my story. My head pounded with every word; at first, I couldn't get the words out, then revelations of incidents connected together by an invisible, yet deadly thread, made their way out of the silent world they had been secretly imprisoned in for over a decade.

'No wonder you're afraid of men', Sister Caris responded compassionately. 'You've been through a lot in your short lifetime!'

As I shared my ordeal it soon became clear I had not run away from the Novice-Mistress, but the voice of yesteryear, accusing, rejecting, despising! Olive Oil unwittingly spoke into all my hidden fears, fears that determined to isolate me for life. I thought I had hated my Novice-Mistress, but I hated my inability to reconcile my principles with my actions; I wanted to love her constantly, but couldn't, I wanted to obey, but something inside wouldn't! I wanted to be 'pure' and all the time, judgement taunted 'defiled', nothing more than a dirty rag to be trodden underfoot. Sister Peter's final demand that I have no social time was the last straw because in isolation, depression would certainly have the victory, and sooner or later, I would have a breakdown. I needed *out*, and I needed to get out quick!

The small clock on the wooden mantelpiece chimed to represent the passing of time as the little balls underneath celebrated with a little dance. 1a.m., all the lights in the convent, except the one we sat under, long switched off, the chill of a winter's night began to bite. Sister Caris was the first to mention the cold.

'I can get us a duvet', I suggested, jumping up and heading toward the bedroom.

'No, it's okay.'

I had learnt in Sociology class at school, many victims of abuse in childhood grow up to become abusers or fall into abusive relationships. I knew I would never become a statistic in either of those groups, but for years, I had fought the fear that others knowing of my past would accuse me of it. From the bedroom door, duvet in hand, I saw the accusation in neon lights flash on-and-off above my head, 'prospective abuser'. Is that what Sister Caris thought of me now?

Reacting to the image in my head of her pointing finger, rather than the kind person sitting on the couch, I defensively offered, 'I can get you your own duvet!'

'No, it's okay', she said with a smile, 'I can share with you.'

We tucked the duvet under our chins and waited for warmth to return to our veins as we continued chatting. This closeness led to another 'hot topic' on my list – why was the pursuit of friendships outside of one's own generation such a big *'no, no'* in the convent? I was angry with everyone else for making me feel so 'ungodly' to want friendship with Sister Caris, but she gave a personal answer.

'For me', she replied, 'when I became a Sister, I gave up the right to become a mother. I must make sure I don't create for myself a replacement for what I've given up to God.'

I could see her logic, but her belief is not one I have ever agreed with. Not that I was looking for a mother figure – no matter how messed-up the rest of my life, that was the one area I was not only content, but grateful! Yet, the mother's number one responsibility is to nurture. The old-fashioned name for the Sister-in-Charge was 'Mother' – maybe, originally, they were given this name because nurturing prioritised above taking charge. While it would be wrong to seek to impersonate the natural bond of mother and daughter, God gives spiritual children to willing hearts to love and to nurture as only a parent can. This means helping them to recognise the path of life Christ has chosen for them and to recognise the potential God has set within them, being a prayer-support in the good times and the bad, rejoicing in their highs and praying God's deliverance in their lows. In it all, praying for their relationship with the Father of Lights to be ever deepened. I wonder what benefits would emerge from this godly role of spiritual parenting being encouraged, rather than avoided, in a communal setting.

I was so grateful for the faithfulness Sister Caris showed in those late night visits, yet, still in the middle of a terrible ordeal I had brought on myself, I worried for everyone's response to me. The Novice-Mistress was miles away from me and yet I still went into panic over how angry she would be. I also wept for the Sisters I desperately missed. In addition, how would Mother Anastasia respond to me when she returns from Holland? Fear gripped me as much as the first day I had entered the Novitiate, only now I had a greater catalogue of error in the file marked 'Unruly Juvenile'.

I returned home to wait for Mother Anastasia's home-coming. On the day she went to Brighton Hall to see the Novice-Mistress, I was to call Sister Caris at 6p.m. to hear the outcome.

'Mother Anastasia is not back yet, ring at seven . . . eight . . . nine . . . ten. She's still not back; ring tomorrow.'

The next day, Sister Caris warned me, 'I'd like to say, "Mother Anastasia is going to give you a tough time, yet everything will be okay", but I can't.'

As she related Mother Anastasia's request I visit in the Mother House on Wednesday, I imagined Mother Anastasia was going to give me a tough time and I was not going to survive! I thought to myself, this is when I find out why some people look afraid in her company. Our relationship will never be the same again! I had given most of my clothes away when I entered the convent, so I wore my sister Pat's white suit, two sizes too big, to the meeting. Petrified, I rang the doorbell. Her assistant, Marie-Therese answering the door, immediately burst out laughing, 'You look like a snowwoman standing there!'

I knew I would not receive such jovial comments from Mother Anastasia! The moments I sat outside her office were some of the longest in history. Eventually, when I was told I could go in, I found Mother Anastasia filing papers away in a large filing cabinet in the corner of her room. Turning her head to me, she smiled, announcing, 'I believe we were in flight at the same time!'

I was shocked to hear her joking, never expecting to hear her dry humour again, especially not today! Her reason for not giving me a hard time, it transpired, was that she couldn't offer me a place in the Novitiate – not yet, at least. Sister Peter, totally shamed by my actions, refused to allow my return (not that I knew whether I wanted to return!). A rule in the Constitution of the Order stated no position be changed within the six months prior to the sexennial Chapter meeting. Having entered that period, Mother Anastasia explained, prevented her appointing a new Novice-Mistress. I could wait until September to re-enter the Novitiate, but as, by then I would have left for over six months, I would have to abide by the rule that states I must begin again! All this too much to consider, especially as I didn't know if I wanted to re-enter, Mother Anastasia offered to arrange for me to live in Community in the Children's Home run by Sister Rose-Anna, receiving 'pocket money' in exchange for work. Ever since Rose-Anna returned to England, our chats on the phone would always turn to her longing for me to be professed *'quickly'* and come to help her manage. Now we didn't need to wait for Profession – how amazing is that!

When I shared the outcome with Yvonne, she was furious. 'Only you . . . Only you could get that response! Anyone else and they'd have said, "Good job we found out in time! We're better off without such trouble." Not you – oh no – they fall over backwards to help you!'

I smiled at her analysis of the situation – they did seem to be extra kind to me when I expected rejection, but I was very glad they chose to act the way they did!☺

14. I Love You with an Everlasting Love

In my meeting with Mother Anastasia, she shared how many Orders send Candidates for assessment before entering the Convent to see if they have a vocation; it wasn't normal for this Order to do so, but would I be willing to go for assessment now?

'It will only work if you are willing to be completely honest.'

I pledged 100% honesty for Mother Anastasia to receive a fair report. Waiting for the arrangements to be made, I meanwhile struggled to come to terms with what I had done. Guilt and an overwhelming sense of unforgiveness toward myself sometimes engulfed me; I knew I was called to forgive *even me*, but was concerned I had affected too many lives. Significant dates etched on my mind pressed heavily upon the nerves of my brain.

Oh, Lord,   *30th January 1987*

Today Brighton Community discusses the Pink Paper! How are O.O and Stevie coping, the shock and trauma of my

hasty, foolish departure weighing even stronger upon their
heartstrings today, as they remember the 'runaway novice's'
'remarkable' answers to the 'Concept of Religious Life'.
Could there ever be a sadder irony! I'm so sorry!

And

Dear Jesus,   *16th February 1987*

Missing the old Sisters has got to be the hardest thing! It's
Lucy's 95th birthday today. How I'd love to see her. The
Sisters' faces only come to me in dreams; my conscious mind
isn't able to see! In the dreams, Dorcas's eyes filling-up with
tears always appear first, then other saddened faces appear,
asking chorally, 'Why?' The pain is too much to bear! If I
left in the 'normal' way, I wouldn't be so anxious for the
Sisters now. I have to face up to what I've done, but how do
I do that? What emotions must I go through before I begin
to see a way out? Fr. McKieran says I will be more mature
because of the experience. Is he right, Lord, or will my
'acting' hinder my growth?

When it was time for me to be assessed, I needed to attend
weekly appointments with a 'Sister Hilarious' in Birmingham
for a month, Sister Caris driving me to the initial meeting.
Emotionally, I could not be expected to handle living in a
new Community and working full time at the same time as
participating in the assessments, so I would join Sr. Rose-Anna
afterwards. In that month, I became very 'private', not even
writing about my experience in my journal, nor did I make a
call to Sister Caris. Mum accused me of *'coming home to shout'*
and I, not usually a violent person, kicked my fourteen-year-
old nephew, only a few years younger than me.

I feel it unforgivable! I'm a hypocrite, preaching the love of Christ and spreading hate. My love must be genuine while I sincerely grow toward You. Going solo in the world is fine, but I can't do this alone, not without You. Draw me to Your living waters for I need to be refreshed. Please!

In the assessments, I was expected to share everything from genealogy to friendships, from public life to the most private thought. On St. Patrick's Day, Mum and I were travelling to Coventry to visit friends. As I had my appointment, I was leaving slightly before my Momma. Before I left, Irish friends of Mum arrived with two shots of whiskey for us to drink, insisting we drink it to celebrate the day with them. Mum, not able to drink 'at that time of morning', insisted I drink both shots. I didn't like whiskey, but in the days when I drank alcohol it had no effect on me – I think I was immune. Mum had never drunk alcohol until she was pregnant with me; she said the pregnancy of her fifth child was so bad, with every problem imaginable, that eventually she followed Doctor's orders to have a 'wee dram' to alleviate the pain! Worrying that my delay arguing with Mum about drinking the whiskey might lead Mum's friends to question why we were travelling separately, I quickly swilled the whiskey down and ran out of the door!

When I arrived with Sister Hilarious, she explained she was going to ask a series of questions I should answer swiftly. What should be the first question on Sister Hilarious's list today?

'Do you drink alcohol?'

'Yes'

'How often do you drink?'

'Occasionally'

'When did you last have a drink?'

'This morning, but . . .'

'No buts! Next question . . .'

Another morning, I was presented with a form full of questions and a pen, and sent into a poky little room (a former broom cupboard, I believe), furnished with a desk and chair, surrounded by off-white walls and no windows. For two hours, I was to answer questions about my life. I must write down in one session, intimacies that might take five years for a person to share with a counsellor. No windows meant I didn't even have the distraction of the mid-day sun to provide a momentary break. As the questions became more and more painful to answer, I wanted to tell Sister Hilarious where to stuff her paper! Yet, reminding myself of the promise I had made to Mother Anastasia to share the truth with this obnoxious woman, I stayed, appearing calm on the outside, turmoil on the inside, answering her deeply intrusive questions.

The ordeal of sharing, however, could not prepare me for the day of reckoning! As Sister Hilarious began sharing her findings, I wanted to scream, *'STOP! You're just repeating what I've told you!'* It was bad enough holding the guilt of voicing deep secrets, but to hear these secrets now spoken, so matter-of-factly as if it was the weather she was reporting – except for that hint of judgement in her voice, hitting her white-washed walls in this clinical environment – was more than I could bear! And what was her final judgement on my suitability as a candidate? In only being able to tell me what I had told her, she didn't know if I had a vocation or merely had close attachments to the Sisters! Stupid Woman! I left her office, fuming, devastated, broken, and more alone than ever – I had travelled through the 'black hole' every Wednesday to get to Sister Hilarious's office, a perilous journey causing carnage within – for what?! I felt my soul had been ripped out and trampled upon. I wanted to curl up and die, but forever needing to hide from my pain, I arrived home and arranged *'the best Mother's Day party ever'*, calling it Mummy's Day Party. The kids were to come in fancy dress, we'd have a talent show, lots of party food and games, and the finale would be finding the Best Dressed Mummy. The rule of the game was simple; the children were to dress their Mummy in toilet-tissue paper head-to-toe, Mum in pink to be dressed by grandson Peter, living with her at the time, and my sisters and sisters-in-law in blue; the best-dressed Mummy would win☺. Everyone really enjoyed that game and right when Momma was all tied up, unable to answer the door, there was a visitor; Sister Caris, on her return journey from visiting her own mother for Mother's Day came to see me. After greeting everyone, I took her up to my room to talk and just had to tell her another story about clothing☺

Having no clothes that fitted me, I was so thrilled when I had the money to buy myself a new outfit, choosing perfectly fitting, smart jean-trousers and top. After I wore them, I washed them (as you do☺) and put them on the line. That evening, as I collected the washing, there was a space where my outfit should have been. At first, I didn't realise what was missing, but when I did I my first thought was concern for the thief's eternal soul (real deep concern!), *'Lord, forgive them, please. Save them from hell'*, I begged. Then living in a poor area, I looked down the hill along the rows of terraced houses below, *'Let my clothes go to the person in most need'*, I confidently asked of my God. I know my selfless response was a result of the 'world' I had come from and the Sisters who shared their principles with me, as, without upset, I was able to release my one and only outfit. Two days later, my Mum's friend, Rita, visiting her mother-in-law, was shown clothes thrown into the garden the night before.

'They look like clothes Kaitlyn was wearing de other day.'

I was so amazed when Rita walked into the house with my outfit! I thought to myself, *All the poor people in this area, and God says I'm the one who needs them most!*'

As Sister Caris looked around my bedroom, she saw escapism, rather than childishness, in my nursery-style version of the sky covering the walls and ceiling, kites flying amidst white and pale-blue clouds, a gigantic rainbow being the main focus of the bedroom, the thick wads of colour taking up a whole wall. At the end of the rainbow, the customary pot of gold replaced, in my world, by a host of teddy bears. A green carpet covered in pink flowers through which to tread carelessly, for no need to fear that they should die, completed my picture of a safe, happy world. OK! Maybe she had a point!☺

'How was your time in Birmingham?' she asked.

At least I could be direct with Sister Caris!

'It was terrible, and I don't want to think about it, let alone talk about it! I'd rather go through the Novitiate a dozen times than ever see that woman again!'

Sister Caris smiled at my extreme comparison, before answering gently,

'Well, it's over now – you'll never have to see her again.'

We turned our thoughts to a happier place – the future and my going to live in Community while I figured out what I wanted to do. Caris offered to meet me at Chester train station and take me across to Rose-Anna in Flint. She would come in the minibus so I could bring the convent bike and she would deliver it safely to its home! Sitting in my imaginary garden with Sister Caris, my little house ransacked past and present, thrown carelessly around by my assessor, yet my future, at least, held hope. Rose-Anna needed my help and I needed to feel useful. Not only that, but Sister Angelina who had cared for me as a volunteer, and through whom God had imbedded a love for Kenya, now lived in the same Community – in listening to stories of her past, I reached out into the unknown, and found promise in my future.

Once there, however, I found it difficult to settle, afraid of *more* failure, yet Holy Spirit spoke into my life all the time. Every scripture we read in the daily prayers seemed to speak into my situation. In a reading from the book of Romans, I felt Jesus assured me I, as a servant of the Lord, would succeed because my Master wants me to succeed, also promising me encouragement and joy brought about by faith. The loving voice of Jesus, however, was always challenged by His vicious competitor, the voice of condemnation roaring in its bid to keep me fastened tightly to guilt and shame, leading me to hide alone in my bedroom for an hour on many evenings, tears rolling out in thunderbolt fashion. Much to my embarrassment, when I returned downstairs, the puffy eyes and blotchy face revealed to everyone, staff and children alike, my private activity.

When my emotions get too bad, a little voice from within calls out, 'Run, run, it's your only escape!' I want to run – run from every problem – but in so doing, I increase the problems. I can't live with me! I can't accept myself! I can't love myself. I can run all over the world, leaving everyone and everything, but one person I can never leave behind, the person I run from is me, and I will always be present!

Whilst I could not return to my past to 'put right' the mistakes of the Novitiate, I continued to try to fast on Wednesdays and Fridays, wanting to overcome *'failure'* in that area at least. Yet, I also continued to *'feast'* on Thursdays and

Saturdays, putting my stomach under great strain. By the time I visited the doctor, blood was flowing out of my back passage with the same vigour as in the front at 'the time of woman'. The doctor insisted I give up fasting for at least six months. I saw this as God's direction and blessing; He only wanted me to be free! Without guilt, I left the habit of fasting behind, for the sake of healing my body. Five years later, in 1992, asking the speaker at a Christian Counselling training day about the relevance of fasting, I realised fear of the damage fasting *might* do to my body had gripped me. The speaker, I believe, spoke as from the mouth of God, 'Katey, it's time for you to begin fasting again.'

I needed to overcome fear to obey what I believe was God's word to me in returning to fasting. When I first fasted, all I knew was Jesus was telling me prayer and fasting go together in interceding for lives and situations. I now experience the blessings of fasting; commanding the demands of 'the flesh' to be quiet that the spirit (the inner-man) may receive understanding from God, while giving me opportunity to draw closer to my Bridegroom, spirit-to-Spirit. There are also certain things in ministry that can only take effect if we are willing to pray and fast. In healing the demon-possessed epileptic boy, for example, Jesus said, 'This type can only come out by prayer and fasting'.[1] Fasting is such an important part of my life in Christ now. Briefly, there are a number of biblical fasts:

- *Full fast*, such as Esther's fast, neither drinking nor eating until the third day, praying for God's protection and direction for the nation of Israel[2]

---

[1] Matthew 17:21
[2] Esther 4:16

- *Liquid fast*, drinking only water, such as Jesus undertook in the desert for 40 days, tempted by the devil, returning in the power of the Spirit, ready to fulfil His commissioning[3]
- *Partial fast*, such as Daniel undertook, eating only basic foods, firstly to remain clean from worldly influence[4] and secondly, to intercede for the nation of Israel[5]

When fasting for a number of days, yet wanting to eat each evening, I believe it is more beneficial to do a partial fast than break the fast nightly – it may sound as if it is the same thing, but on a partial fast, you are more likely to limit your food intake, and remain in a spiritually 'receptive' mode. Putting our trust in God is more important than anything. Fasting never damaged my body, but the gluttony surrounding it did. Therefore, I must trust God to train me in coming off the fasts not to 'pig-out', for my God provides my every need. He gives me all the nutrients I need to live a healthy life, in spirit, soul and body.

In 1987, my *'year of devastation'*, God's primary concern was to make me secure in His love, no matter my mistakes. After prayers one evening, I imagined Rose-Anna standing up to close the open window behind us. My reaction was to gleefully announce, *'I knew you were going to do that before you did it.'*

Jesus immediately spoke into my heart, *'I knew you were going to run away and I loved you! Why should my feelings change now? In knowledge of your faults and failings, I loved you! I will always love you!*

---

[3] Luke 4:2, 14

[4] Daniel 1:8–17

[5] Daniel 9:3

I feel peace and happiness in Your affirmation, Lord, that seeing my darker side, You are able to love me, but I know I also need to love myself and accept love from others. I have a long journey to travel. Lead me, dear Lord!

God's affirmation was also expressed in a letter from a beloved Sister in Brighton Hall:

My dear Kaitlyn,

Thank you ever so much for your sweet little letter which confirmed the sad news that you have left us . . . I said to the Lord, 'Did you really take her from us, dear Lord?' He did not answer me, so we best leave it to Him. He might just change His mind yet some day and then you will be most welcome back . . . Now my dear, don't worry, but trust and love the Lord. He will never leave you. Let's pray for each other.

Yours, Sister Dorcas

Mother Anastasia came to visit on my birthday to talk with me before she should meet Sister Hilarious the next day. I told her to expect negative results. 'She only looks for problems, so that's all she's going to find!'

I was most upset, sharing how Sister Hilarious made me feel like a 'crackpot', suggesting I needed counselling. Mother Anastasia thought rather than counselling, I needed to attend a college course to help me see my positive side – *I hope she's paying!*☺

Sister Hilarious also saw me as a born-leader who refused to lead. It wasn't for selfish reasons I wouldn't lead, but to save humanity from another bad leader! I simply wasn't kind or gentle enough to be what I perceived to be a good leader.

I did decide, however, I wanted to implement another of Sister Hilarious' recommendations; prove my 'stickability' by continuing something for two years before I consider re-entering the Novitiate. Mother Anastasia initially offered work in any of their Convents (although unmentioned, that probably excluded Brighton☺). To my request I remain in the Children's Home, working with Rose-Anna, Mother Anastasia said she would ask Father McKieran's permission. That same evening, a new acquaintance, Steve, arrived at the door with a birthday card and gift, asking if I could come out for an hour, inviting me to a prayer meeting.

I went to the prayer meeting last night with Steve. He forgot to tell me the group is an all-male one. You have a sense of humour, Lord. Imagine me, one of the lads! ☺

The next day I phoned Sister Caris, sharing how everyone was reading 'romance' into my new relationship, yet I was happy with friendship.

'That's right', she said. 'Take one step at a time.'

'Besides', I replied, 'I can't go out with anyone when I'm probably going to return to Religious Life. How would that be when I say, "See ya', I'm going back to the Convent now"'!

Here, Sister Caris disagreed with me, suggesting guilt and fear led me to race ahead.

'Take your time'; she pleaded, 'live one day at a time.'

I didn't like what I was hearing because I knew she was right! I was afraid of getting into a close relationship. Caris thought a relationship would make me feel more human, lovable, 'someone special'.

'I told you God would bring someone into your life', she shared excitedly, before laughing. 'I just didn't think it would be so quick!'

A couple of days later I was invited, along with 'my Community' to Jubilee celebrations in Chester.

Dear Jesus,   *01.05.87*

*I've had a lovely night! It was wonderful – full of You, Lord, for You are Love! I saw a few sisters for only minutes. Conversation dried up beyond, 'How are you?' Still it was nice to see them. Sister Caris apologised in front of Mother Anastasia for not sending my birthday card, **'Your best friend forgot you!'** Lord, what does she and Mother Anastasia really think of me feeling that way? Is it a joke to them – **'She'll get over it'** – or can friendship exist regardless of age? I believe so.*

*For a girl who feels more secure in women's company, I was socialising rather well with the men! Three Seminarians I had studied with were there, so I spent a good while with them. I'm getting into this **'all-lads together'** stuff! (Thank You, Lord!) I really enjoyed Fr. McKieran (whom I'm ever so fond of) and Fr. Watson's company; they both ridicule me (in a harmless way). Their humour is so quick. I was blushing for ages! They're really lovely. And Fr. McKieran said I can work with Rose-Anna; my official starting date being tomorrow, so that's great! Goodnight now, Lord* ☺

Now I had a job, the next thing was to find a home☺. Travelling by bus, as Rose-Anna and I passed the most notorious estate in the area I told her I would happily live there. Rose-Anna gasped in horror. 'It's so dangerous'

'God'll protect me! It would be great – I'd be right in the thick of it, with plenty of opportunity to bring Jesus into the situation.'

Rose-Anna, in fear for my 'foolishness', almost dropped to her knees right there on the bus, asking God to protect me from myself! Her inner-prayer was answered before we got home, the Cheshire Society having rung to say they had a flat available across the road from the Children's Home. Both Rose-Anna and Steve accompanied me for the viewing and were amazed; climbing stairs around a church steeple conjured-up mystical stories in our imaginations. The adjoining church was long demolished, but the locals refused to lose the steeple as a landmark in the local landscape. Inside, the flat was not only immaculate, but fitted with expensive carpets, curtains and lampshades. The last occupant had died without family. Her friends had removed the furniture, but thought the next tenant would benefit from the fittings.

Thank You, Lord, for giving me such a beautiful flat; the pink bathroom sealed it for me – this is my new home! The word 'my' is so important to me, talking of 'belonging'. That's why I always say, 'my sisters' – I want to belong!

Steve and I again spent some time together that evening,

He asked me to become his girlfriend. I said 'yes'. My tummy is a little churned-up now. I'm afraid of close relationships. I feel its right, so stay close please Lord! Bless us both. I don't know how to be. I never want to spend a lot of time with a person, so I don't know how this will work out. Over to You, Lord!

A few weeks later, Steve suggested a romantic picnic down by the lake, but romance doesn't bloom naturally when the lady has an infection in one eye. I felt like a pirate! Throughout the summer, we continued to go along to the prayer meeting in which God's peace was so tangible. In the calm of a quiet moment, a verse came to me,

I wanted to run a hundred miles, running from my life.
I ran a million miles and found my destiny.

Confidence filled my being that everything was okay with God. He was with me every step of the way, regardless of what He would have chosen for me. I also saw a picture of me carrying a wardrobe. Although it was heavy, carrying the wardrobe brought about a rewarding feeling, pride at being able. I saw this as a sign that God was taking care of my worldly needs (like all the furniture needed for my new home) and that spiritual gifts awaited me. Within no time at all, furniture began to come from all directions. The following week as I visited with a friend, snuggling in her plush pink chair, thoughts of my new home filled my mind,

I want to live alone with You, my Lover. I want to be comfortable in Your love. I looked at Eva's pink suite and asked You for my own pink suite. Half of me objected, asking You not to listen to my desires. However, I felt the answer to be 'Yes, you can have all the material wealth you want, but you have to be willing to give it all back.' 'I'll remember that, Lord, I promise', I replied. Immediately, I began to wonder how and when I would find my pink suite, but Your promise doesn't surprise me. The God of surprises is a very generous God! You really are spoiling me with many bouquets. Thank You, Jesus. Teach me to respond with a generous heart.

Within days, I spotted my pink suite advertised in the local newspaper and hours later, was arranging it in my living room. Beautiful!☺ I was in a state of euphoria in my life coming together; job, home, boyfriend, I was even about to begin driving lessons! I visited the Sisters in Brighton in this elated state. The Sisters, welcoming and loving me, could not understand my new life or my ecstasy. Perhaps, I had moved too quickly into this 'other world'! Some Sisters shared the upset of that night Sister Celia announced, 'The novice has left.' Receiving no explanation was the most confusing part for them, their thoughts keeping them awake, running back and forth to the bathroom, until Sister Celia shouted in her commanding Scottish accent, 'Go to bed now! I don't want to hear another person out on this corridor till morning!'

Sister Peter was away when I visited. Although seeing her would have 'frightened' me, I would also have liked the opportunity to try to be reconciled. Yet, when I arrived, I realised I had not considered another important relationship that needed reconciliation through my apology – to Sister Celia, for what I had put her through! Perhaps, the Lord considered one act of reconciliation enough for my first visit with 'my Sisters'! I believed, albeit privately, one day Christ would also reconcile Sister Peter and me. My visit, however, was primarily to visit the elderly Sisters. Having stayed only two days, I wrote to Jesus,

I don't mind shedding a few tears for loss of my beloved Sisters, but I know it to be exactly right. Thank You for allowing me to come and allowing me to go!

Arriving back to my little flat, two letters waited for me on the mat, both with handwriting I recognised. Momma asked, *'Was there great joy at Brighton Hall, everyone welcoming you, or did they tell you to get on your bike?'*

Sister Caris also made light of my escape, sending a card with a drawing of a bike. The message read, *'The road goes in many directions. Whichever path you choose to take, you will be happier if you follow your heart.'* Sister Caris added, *'And make sure the lights are working!☺'*

Within weeks, I was with 'my Sisters' at Rescue for the annual Garden Party, although I had long admitted I no longer belonged. My arm linked with a guy probably proved that point! I found Sister Caris' greeting so amusing – 'Pleased to meet you, Steve; I've put you on the bouncy castle – oh, no, the train.'

So that was us parted until the end of the day. Mother Anastasia, on meeting Steve, said, 'I've heard a lot about you, Steve. Flint's existence depends on you – or at least, Kaitlyn's does!' (What a character!☺)

Father McKieran, on the other hand, completely ignored Steve! I never knew if this was because he thought I was rushing too quickly into things or his reaction was simply part of the package of him 'having a bad day'. He was always protective toward me, something I very much appreciated – a Big Daddy figure☺. If he did have concerns about my relationship with Steve, he could join the queue. My mother was petrified I would rush into marriage. Still hoping I would re-enter the Convent, she insisted, 'You're not ready for marriage!'

When I was in the Convent, she had shared, 'I'm so glad you've become a nun. I don't have to worry about you being treated badly by any husbands.' (You can see where her brokenness lay!)

I too had great reservations about this relationship. For one thing, Steve wanted to move too fast. He was quickly 'brandishing' those three special words around while I coldly refused to believe it. How could it be true; he didn't know me long enough to love me! He also longed to hear those words come lovingly from my lips, but with my feet firmly on the ground, I refused to 'gush out' words that did not come from the heart! I had also told Steve abuse was in my past, yet gave no details. As the months went on, this Christian boyfriend wanted to move toward a more intimate relationship, and my 'unwillingness to accept my sexual identity' was blamed for holding us back.

If the world was a stage and my life a play, I would like to shout 'STOP', and as director, question this whole scenario. My sexual hang-ups (which I definitely had) should not have actually affected our pre-marital relationship as sex according to God's word is for the marriage bed, and nowhere else! Christians are to deal with their hang-ups in counselling or in prayer but definitely not in sin. I am so glad I was not led into 'accepting my sexual identity' through pressure to become more intimately involved. I have to say here, as a Christian, Steve also did not condone sex before marriage. Yet what constitutes 'sex'? It is not only sexual intercourse, but every activity that sexually arouses you. When these arousals are illegitimate (outside of the undefiled marriage bed), we are told as Christians to protect ourselves by fleeing. I didn't understand fully then, but I thank God that He used my fear to keep me from entering in any deeper, and after five months, the relationship having become all too much for me, I bade our romantic liaison farewell.

I thank God for the brief romance God gave over a decade later when I had received an abundance of healing into my *whole* identity! I don't remember the exact time when God told me to stop dating guys simply because they were interested in me; my likes and dislikes were important too!

'What would you like in a husband?' Jesus asked.

A man similar to the one I described first became a good friend before we began 'seeing one another'. I had just received deep, deep sexual healing, in which love of being a 'woman' replaced lifetime resentment at not being born a man. What I needed in my healing was not 'activity', but 'pure love', no crossing over the boundaries set by God's Word! God's healing made me 'feel like a virgin', just like the song says, except, as God's princess, I was not to be 'touched for the very first time' before marriage. Even Edward received a direct warning from our Heavenly Father, *'Be careful how you treat My daughter!'* No 'love in braille' as I heard one preacher say recently! Edward also needed healing from racial abuse, lies that claimed he was not the white man's equal; therefore, no white woman would entertain thoughts of entering relationship with him. After a few weeks, however, God showed us this pure, undefiled relationship, was not the long-term one to which we would each be called. We easily returned to being 'just friends' as I requested an agreement with Jesus, *'I don't want to go on as much as one date until You introduce me to the man You have chosen as my husband.'* Since then, another decade has passed and I am better off for not entering into any wrong, and therefore, wasteful relationships. Am I upset to be alone? When a friend came to visit, she commented, 'I know there are no humans living here with you, but it's hard to imagine you alone; the way you speak to Jesus it's as if He lives here in Person.'

In the Novitiate, I once wrote in my journal,

*If I make the decision to be **alone** I can expect to be **lonely**, but if I decide to be **alone with You**, I can expect to **be loved**!*

God's promises are *always* worth waiting for and in waiting on God, we get to be loved – what a great deal! ☺

15. My Presence Will Go with You and I Will Give You Rest

You've just had a little glimpse of the 21st Century Katey and the wonderful healing I have received from my Lord and Saviour, but back to 1987! The conflicting feelings regarding my past still fought within me,

So much hope, so much despair! Materially, I'm settled. Emotionally, I'm a wanderer. I want one day to be settled within myself – when I reach that place, please let it be forever! Isaiah writes,

Yes, Yahweh will have pity on Jacob, He will choose Israel once more and settle them in their own country.

(see Isaiah 14:1 NJB)

Thank You, Lord. Settle me within my own country, within my own self, not looking to others to find the answers, but finding the answers to life within me.

Visits with Sister Caris were rare times in which I would release so much pain, trusting her enough to cry – weep buckets, in fact! I never felt healed, but I did feel relief. I could not believe the good points she credited me with but in believing she was genuine in saying them, I began to believe I was loved (this belief would waver, but it was there!)

Loneliness can take a long time to heal, and Jesus, not anything superficial, is the Healer!

For as long as I could remember, I had enjoyed my own company. As a child, if I returned to an empty home, instead of the noisy, bustling one it was renowned for being, I'd respond ecstatically, revelling in 'time alone' at home. Now, with the 'cat out of the bag', I could barely stand to be alone, afraid of my own thoughts. I would visit friends until 1a.m. even though I might need to be in work by 7a.m. I might talk Sister Caris or Fr. McKieran's ear off for two hours in an evening. Sometimes, I would run to the Children's Home, desperately despairing of life. A hive of activity, so many characters, so many issues and needs to turn my focus away from 'self', giving my inner-man space and time to adjust, finding its own 'even-keel', would save the day. Depression, however, would sometimes grip me too strongly for me to turn to people. I remember in those two years of 'sticking it out', wandering aimlessly through streets late at night, even in the rain, lost, uncertain, and most emphatically, hopeless! Yet, Christ's comfort always seemed to find a way in, lifting my head once again, filling me with hope of a healed and purposeful future, for 'weeping may endure for a night, but joy comes in the morning'.[1]

In September, Sister Rose-Anna and I went back to school. As well as working full time and beginning the Social Care

---

[1] Psalm 30:5b

course, I enrolled in 'A level' Theatre class. My purpose was to combine my love of drama with the childcare I had always wanted to do. I was also nearing the end of my driving lessons, so I had a lot to be grateful for. I could still reach pitiful lows, but I began to have more 'good days' than bad. When the date arrived for what would have been my Profession, I was able to find peace.

I feel no guilt, no remorse and no upset. My life is here. When I look back, I rejoice in the good times. When I remember the bad times, sometimes I can see growth, and if not, I rejoice in my escape and present freedom. The break had to come sometime, and suppressing my emotions as I did, that break had to be dramatic! For today, at least, I'm totally content in my life. I've been this happy before, but not this content. I've never been as settled. I see you've answered my prayer in many ways – I'm not as sensitive as I was. I have more confidence. I've found a purpose. I have goals. I'm mobile – and I adore travel!

In January, I faced the first anniversary of my 'escape' head-on by visiting Brighton. Sister Caris having moved there was an absolute 'Godsend' for me, giving me the freedom to express myself, sharing my experiences of loneliness and pain. She also was willing to laugh at my memories of situations, helping me to throw away the pain, that it no longer affect me. I shared how, when I asked for driving lessons as a postulant, I was refused.

'No, no, no!' Sister Celia informed me. 'We don't arrange driving lessons for postulants and novices!'

Just as well they didn't, or I might have 'borrowed' the convent car instead of the convent bike!

Collecting Rose-Anna from the 'Rescue convent' weeks later was not so positive an experience. It started pleasantly enough; Bridie, as down to earth as the potatoes she peeled every day, smiled as she saw me approaching the kitchen entrance. Her wet hands immersed in a sink-full of dishes were soon wiped dry on her work apron as she headed toward me to give a thousand welcomes, 'Kaitlyn, it's so good to see you!'

Although not a nun, Bridie seemed to have more right to be in the Convent than the Sisters stationed in it, having been around 'forever' and working morning till night, all but sleeping there! Always 'on the go', Bridie was soon heading out the door, 'I have to go do a bit of cleaning in Fader's house. I'll see you again.'

As Bridie sped off on her old-fashioned, heavy steel bike, an uncomfortable silence descended on the elderly Sisters left in the kitchen. In their day, any novice leaving was secretly ushered out the back door never to be spoken of again. They didn't quite know how to deal with a runaway novice standing in their kitchen! Waiting for Rose-Anna to 'finish off', I too began to feel uncomfortable. As Sister Reba made herself a cuppa, I looked at the back door where the 'beggars' always came for a drink and sandwich. One man always asked for Sister Reba. One day, as a postulant, I came to the dining room door and shouted through to the community room in my 'Irish accent', *'Sister Reba, your man's at the door!'*

She tittered at the insinuation, 'Ooh! Ooh! My man!'

I wished something funny could happen now to break the uncomfortable silence! Fr. McKieran, thank God, saved the day! Swinging open the door from the office, holding a glowing reference in one hand and a bottle of champagne in the other, he greeted me with a friendly hug.

*The hug I wanted more than anything! I would have liked to
hug him back, but I'm too shy*☺

When it came to Fr. McKieran's jubilee, I really did not
want to go! With every mile we drove a little closer to the
celebrations, I wound-up the 'clock-work comedian' – just one
more turn – ready for action! Mother Anastasia, in greeting
me, held my face, only for seconds, but enough to assure me
of her love and acceptance. I expressed all the security I could
from the comfortable relationship I had with 'Mother and
Father'. He, as always, was so special in the way he related to
me, which in turn made me feel guilty for not wanting to be
there! None of these emotions was on the surface, though –
the show must go on and so peals of laughter travelled the
corridors of the Convent as I shared my funny stories. Alone
in my little flat later that night, the 'wall of wit' temporarily
laid down, I was safe once again to share my true feelings with
the One who cares.

Dear Jesus,

*Today was horrible! I don't like being with the
'Congregation' at functions. A nod and a smile to all the
Sisters – telling the ones who always ask and then forget –
'No, I'm not a novice, but I used to be' – that's the crux –
'**I don't belong, but I used to.**' Jesus, I want to run away,
not be faced with all that!*

With my emotions so 'up and down', sometimes I found
life 'just so hard!' A Sister sometimes stayed over from another
convent, studying 'Counselling' in a nearby college. We spent
time together, one thing led to another and before long, I was
her 'guinea pig'! Her counsel was helpful to begin with; I felt

relief, but with strange techniques, like playing in a sand tray (she really does think I'm a guinea pig!☺), and with her infatuation in believing I was seeking a mother-figure in my relationship with Sister Caris, sessions with her soon piled on guilt instead of relieving me of negative feelings. My solution was to avoid her! Meanwhile, my Momma's love had a stabilising effect in the midst of my whirlwind of emotions. She proved her worthiness of the title carried in my heart, *'Best Mum in the world'*, when I rang one day and asked, 'Can you come?'

No questions asked to verify the urgency of my request. 'I'll see what time the next coach leaves.' What a treasure!☺

I drove the three-hour journey home whenever I could to receive affirmation through shared cuddles and laughter, yet my inability to verbalise the war within me – didn't she have enough to suffer! – hindered any real progress. In the Social Care class, we would occasionally have different professionals present the value of their career and experience to us.

Mr. Dutch, take centre stage!

Mr. Dutch, an ex-vicar, was a counsellor speaking at the end of our academic year in the summer of 1988, and as he spoke, I warmed toward him, perceiving he was a genuinely nice man. Back in Brighton, one of the Sisters', Fredrick, blinded through diabetes, was always trying to perceive the goings-on of convent life with her ears, more often than not assuming incorrectly, resulting in wild accusations that repeatedly led her into 'hot water'. My saving grace in establishing 'safe' relationships was a God-given gift of discernment; being a good discerner of character enabled me to fight my fears when I might otherwise take flight (again!) In the year-and-a half after leaving the convent it had become blatantly clear to me that Sister Hilarious had been right on the issue of my needing counselling, and although Sister Trainee Counsellor had not been able to help me, maybe this 'good man' could.

On my first visit, I only shared that my father had left the family home when I was five, my sister and her two children had died tragically when I was seven, and I had run away from the convent. I had not even skimmed the surface, yet Mr. Dutch responded in saying I had a lot to work through!

He hopes I don't chicken out. I'm used to pain, ain't I? I couldn't imagine packing it in, but who knows how I might react after months of intensity!

On that same evening, I recorded,

No one will ever know how much my 'acting' saves me. Tonight, I could have had a nervous breakdown if I didn't frighten myself and in that fear, turn my actions into rehearsals of drama techniques.

On my second visit with Mr. Dutch (Harry),

I shared how I cut people off, expecting rejection. I don't believe people can accept me as I am. I find it difficult to share myself and expect people's patience to wear thin. (I expect it of your man. He says he'll never reject me. We'll see! It's only a test – ONLY! I'm hooking my life on that guy! He better not reject me, not even slightly!)

On my third visit,

We talked about Sister Caris, and 'b'gora', he understood – the first person ever! He said he saw two poles, one of

*despair (the slime I see within myself) and the other, a
pole of hope, in which I can see my own character in Sister
Caris.*

The greatest sigh of relief in history bubbled forth from
my lips. After a session with Sister Trainee-Counsellor, months
before, had I not written the same in my journal in defence
of loving Sister Caris! Without confidence in your own
thoughts, however, you don't truly believe you have the right
to assert them. To hear the same words from a counsellor is
more than confirmation; it is licence to believe what you
already know to be true! I was learning to love myself by
loving similar characteristics in Sister Caris. It was true, her
faithfulness to me beyond duty, and my desire to be like her,
had placed her on a pedestal for a time. Yet, as I began to deal
with the *'dung'* in my life, I realised the *'yucky'* feelings were
not 'me', but a response to events. In recognising my personality had similar characteristics to Sister Caris, then, hey, I was
beginning to see God has not done a bad job! Deep down, I
am lovable too!☺

With Harry's help, I began to deal with issues from
childhood that for years I had only viewed through the eyes
of a child, taking responsibility for every evil that happened.
When I prepared for my First Holy Communion, my understanding of Jesus' death was that if I had not done naughty
things, He would not have had to die. (I *alone* was responsible
for Christ's death!) Six months before I met Harry I had
written in my journal that Jesus was leading me into the
freedom of Christianity, guiding me to release myself from
the bonds of guilt. Yet, when I met Harry a great weight of
responsibility still lay on that little girl's shoulders and with
his help, I began to unravel my past to see what parts I was
responsible for and what parts I wasn't.

It was God's timing, I am sure, that by the end of August, having seen Harry a number of times, I had worked through my feelings about the Novitiate and my escape. I drove to collect Rose-Anna after her retreat in the Mother-house, but was I in for a shock! O.O – Sister Peter – was there, back *only one hour* from sabbatical in Rome! Talk about God's timing! I knew I must take the opportunity, asking to speak to her after lunch. We went into a room to be alone. I thought she was rather superficial in her communication and maybe she sensed it, all of a sudden speaking directly, 'No, I have no ill-feelings about what happened, none of it, and I'm sure you were spontaneous in your decision. Believe me, Love, I genuinely mean that!'

I couldn't help but believe her – never had I heard her call me, 'Love'! She shared how she had received healing in Rome (which I'm sure is a main reason she went there). I nervously allowed her a glimpse inside the person I refused to reveal whilst her 'charge', explaining how the way I left made me face myself; what a painful year it had been, but how much better I was now feeling, even though there was still so much to sort out. She said she had thought of me often in Rome, just as I had thought of her often – it brought a strange sense of a bond; in forgiveness, we had found acceptance. Our chat brought closure for both of us, never to be in relationship again; we had found peace, at last, united in Christ's love.

After my two-year commitment, I still was not ready to return to the Convent,

I think of the Franciscans as my Sisters and yet I cannot be with them. I have to experience healing before thinking about returning 'home'. I must find happiness within myself before I seek community-life. I want only to be close to You,

Lord, so I'll seek You first, leaving all other human contact aside.

Wanting, in the meantime, to 'live the dream' I found work in America for a year. Leaving England, my two-year-old question, did I have a vocation or did I simply have a close bond to the Sisters, was still unanswered. Little did I know that on arriving in New York, the answer would come as quick as a flash! A nun walked by in the airport. In England, I would have taken a second look to see if she was 'one of ours', but knowing this was unlikely, my subconscious lifted its voice to the surface, *'I could never be a nun!'* I immediately accepted that thought to be direction from God. This revelation, however, does not indicate that Jesus never called me to the Convent. I gained a rich foundation in those years that I shall forever remain grateful for! I found wonderful role-models in a number of Sisters. And as for those relationships I found difficult, being 'stretched' in behaviour and attitude is good for any of us! I also would not have faced up to my need for Jesus' healing except my emotions were 'pushed to the brink'. Yet, the greatest benefit of my 'formative years' was the opportunity to spend so much time alone with my Lord and Saviour, Jesus Christ. My favourite part of 'ministry' today is entering God's presence to minister to Him alone – without my 'formative years' being primarily alone with Jesus, I doubt I'd recognise the call, let alone answer it!

. . . The years have flown by from that day to this. Following the call of God on my life has remained of central importance to me. Only months after I began a personal relationship with Father God in September 1991, He asked me to undertake the most dramatic change of my life, leaving the Catholic Church.

My new circle of friends and acquaintances were soon formed primarily in non-denominational fellowships, whilst two close friendships in the Catholic Church were maintained. For almost a decade, however, my only contact with the Convent I'd left behind was occasional correspondence with a few Sisters. Ministering in Kenya in 1999 and 2007, I was able to visit with the Sisters living there, including Bernice, the fun-loving nun whom I had worked alongside in a Children's Home in my volunteers' year. Moving to Ireland in 2008 brought the opportunity to re-establish friendships from my Brighton years, yet, in September 2009, God surprised me when I was quickly passing through the city that He instructs me to call Ireland's 'Jerusalem'.

Without any intention of visiting the Sisters there, the Lord asked me, 'Would you go to Yorkshire without visiting your family?'

I didn't understand why He should ask such a question, but answered, 'No.'

Jesus then asked, 'Then why are you passing through without seeing your family here?'

I was amazed – and thrilled – to hear after my leaving, not only the convent, but also the Catholic Church, my God still calls these dear, precious Sisters *'my family'!* Being the great Organiser that He is, the day I visited, Sisters from convents throughout Ireland were meeting together for a Reflection Day. God strengthened friendships with Sisters I had known all those years ago whilst forming new relationships for the Twenty-First Century. Attempting to live my life divinely led by Christ, I was at the beginning of a new era, having just arranged my *first* Conference *ever* to be held two months later. As the speaker at the Reflection Day referred to a Scripture in Isaiah, I read it in my Bible, then felt led to read a corresponding verse:

Go through,
Go through the gates!
Prepare the way for the people,
Build-up,
Build-up the highway!
Take out the stones,
Lift up a banner for the peoples!

(Isaiah 62:10)

Right there, amongst *'my Sisters'*, 26th September 2009 in the natural, far beyond time or space in the spiritual realm; the vastness I used to view through Brighton's chapel window alone with my God in the comfort of dark, wintry nights, broke through every feasible barrier, brightening as it moved closer toward me, entering my heart with enough force to bowl me over!

'Will you come, will you obey?' the voice of my Lord and Saviour asked.

'Yes, Lord, I'll follow You wherever You lead!'

Commissioned to serve in Ireland, I received a warning not to despise small beginnings. The one conference already arranged would be the beginning of 'something so BIG'. In the following year, little did I know, God's 'small beginnings', would include *little, tiny, totally unknown me,* ministering in 14 Irish towns and cities, arranging and speaking at 9 Conferences, preceded by 42 days of intercession and prayer-walking, alongside 36 days of evangelism, working with Christians from 42 churches in 14 counties north, south, east and west of Ireland. I'm glad God wasn't planning anything big,☺ but seriously, we serve a God of impossibilities and for every divine commission, there is God's provision!

Another significant occurrence of the day was when a gently spoken eighty-two-year-old averted World War 3's eruption!

One Sister had asked the speaker what she thought of people who leave their 'first calling'. Everyone presuming she was speaking of leaving the priesthood or convent, reacted angrily, wanting to protect those attending the day, who like me, had previously been a Sister with them. The emotional temperature rose dramatically as each person spoke and anyone would wonder where it was all going to end!

When all had their say, this wise, gentle lady I refer to spoke up, 'The way I see it is your first calling is to love Jesus. If you leave the priesthood or convent, but continue to love and follow Jesus, then you are not leaving your "first call".'

A blanket of peace descended upon the attendees, and without knowing the Sister's name, I said, 'Lord, there's a lady I'd like to spend time with; I'd like to glean from her wisdom!'

God is good, so kind and faithful, in answering our prayers, giving me a number of opportunities during my travels in Ireland to spend time with Sister Jay-Kelly☺. As my relationship with the Sisters has always been 'an adventure', let me finish my story of my experience of 'Convent living' with a recent escapade during a visit to the Sisters.

Only one Sister was at home when I asked to use the washing machine out in the laundry behind the house. As I passed the kitchen, I put a pan on the stove. Returning from the laundry, I found the back door to the house locked; Sister Susan had locked me out! I began to bang and shout, although I knew if she was in her bedroom at the front of the house, she would have little chance of hearing me. Then I noticed her shopping note was missing from the dining-room table; Sister Susan was no longer in the house! If I hadn't put the pan on the stove, I would simply have waited for her to come back, but I *had* put the pan on the stove! I looked through the kitchen window at the pan – no steam yet. I must find a way out of the walled garden and make my way to the local shops to retrieve the key from Sister Susan.

Peering over the wall, seeing the conservatory door of the house to my left was open, I began to shout, 'Hello! Hello!' No answer.

The family had obviously been decorating, having left a tray containing a roller and wooden spoon on their shed roof. I took the spoon and stretched over to bang on the kitchen window. The only response I got was from the dog, barking wildly. Deciding to climb over the wall to get the attention of the neighbours, I ran to the other side of the garden to drag over the large wheelie bin for me to climb up on to, checking the pan as I passed the window. Now it was boiling! I climbed on the wall, putting one foot on the shed, but being one of those lightweight plastic affairs, it began to come away at the seams, so I quickly put my foot on the windowsill and jumped down onto the garden path. Entering the conservatory, I called, 'Hello', only to realise the door was open to let in a little fresh air for the dog. I took a ladder standing by the shed and ran to the wall of the next house, shouting, 'Hello, anyone there.'

I climbed over, but again no one was home. I had reached the end of the row of houses, so I climbed back over the first wall, and then ran to the second wall with the open ladders and climbed over yet again, back into the Convent garden. Now the food was burned and I was sure the fire alarm was about to be triggered. What would Sister Jean, the present Mother General say? (Although, she has a more modern title that I don't remember.)

'Katey, you are forbidden to visit our Convents!'

By this time, concern turned to anxiety! I rolled the bin to the right side of the garden and began to call out, 'Hello! Hello!'

Seeing I was getting no response, I began to shout, 'Help! Help!'

The neighbour next-door-but-one came to her bathroom window. 'What's wrong?' she asked.

As I was explaining, I saw the Sisters' next-door neighbour appear at her bedroom window. I waved her to come downstairs. She sauntered through the kitchen and into the garden and calmly asked, 'Yes?'

I quickly explained I was a visitor (and hoped she wouldn't mistake me for a burglar!), how Sister Susan had inadvertently locked me out and I had left a pan on the stove, *'which I'm sure is about to set off the fire alarm'*.

'See!' I screamed, as I heard the first bells ringing. 'Can I come through your house to find Sister?'

'Sure', she agreed, waving the way.

Exasperated, I looked at the long drop. 'Do you have a stool or chair I can step down on?'

She came with a tiny stool and put it on the path rather than on the soil near the wall. To reach it I would need to do the long jump! When I was at school, I could never do gymnastics very well, especially jumping over the 'wooden horse', as I was too small and fat, but on that day, even I was amazed at the 'flight' fright can achieve! I bounced off the Sisters' wheelie bin, cart wheeling over the wall, heading beyond the tiny stool, on to the path. I then ran through her home only to be confused by the layout of the house and the multitude of doors. Turning back, I called, 'Which way is your front door?'

Opening an adjoining door, the neighbour pointed the way. I ran down the street, hoping Susan was in the nearest shop. Yes! She was approaching the till with a few items resting in her arms.

'You've locked me out', I screeched. 'Give me your key.'

Susan handed me the tomato in her right hand, presumably freeing that hand to reach for the key but then calmly asserted, 'I didn't lock you out. I gave you a key.'

'You locked me out the back. I left a pan on the stove and now the fire alarm is going off. I need to get in and switch it off.'

'You don't know the number.'

'I don't mean the alarm! I need to switch off the stove! Give me the key!!!'

Susan handed me another tomato. I grabbed the few items held between her two arms, totally freeing her, dropping them on the till beside us, before reaching out my hand.

'Give me the key!'

(I'm not excusing my curt behaviour, but I really did think, by this point, I was going to be in such major trouble with Sister Jean!) Having obtained the key, I ran across the road (even without looking!) but with backless sandals on, I was just too slow. I stopped, removed them and ran full-pelt to the Convent.

'Now, I'm truly African', I said to myself, imagining running alongside all those great Kenyan female athletes☺. I let myself into the Convent, alarm ringing, house full of smoke, pan ruined, but no major damage done.

In saunters Susan and laughs before saying, 'Do you know who you reminded me of when you came running and screeching into the shop? Manuel from Fawlty Towers!'

I laughed, she was absolutely right; my voice had risen a few octaves, and my arms were flying all over the place, but I hadn't burnt the house down, and hopefully, 'my Sisters' will still allow me to visit☺.

Useful Information

Ellel Ministries, a non-denominational Christian ministry, was set up in England in 1986 to bring God's healing love to those who are struggling with life's issues and to provide extensive training for those seeking to minister effectively to others. It is now established in over 20 countries around the world including Ireland, Australia and America. Contact can be made with any of the bases through the International Headquarters:

> Ellel Ministries
> Ellel Grange,
> Bay Horse, Lancaster,
> LA2 0HN, United Kingdom
>
> http://www.ellelministries.org

Christian Radio in Ireland:

UCB Ireland http://www.ucbirelandradio.com or Satellite: channel 0214

UCB is an inter-denominational radio station presenting teaching, discussions and daily devotions, playing only Christian music, including the best of Irish Christian music.

A prayer-line is available Monday to Friday, 9.30a.m. – 10.30p.m., call 1 890 940 300

Spirit Radio http://www.spiritradio.ie/ on FM in many cities, nationwide on 549 Medium Wave

Upbeat and uplifting, entertaining and inspirational, Spirit Radio plays contemporary Christian music – plus a selection of positive mainstream hits. Presenters highlight stories that show how faith in God makes a real difference, aiming to reach across community divides – to listeners in homes, cars and offices – with a selection of music and talk programming that is both encouraging and fresh.

Life FM Radio, Cork http://www.lifefm.ie

The aim of LifeFM is to provide Cork's Christian Community with a unique, family-friendly radio station that reflects the ups and downs of real life, while presenting music and pro-gramming that maintains Christian family values.

Shine FM-102.4 FM http://tunein.com/radio/Shine-FM

102.4 Shine FM is a community based charity radio station, with a strong Christian ethos. The station broadcasts 24 hours a day to Banbridge Town and the surrounding areas in County Down, Northern Ireland and to the rest of the world on the web.